Short Introduction to Corporate Finance

The *Short Introduction to Corporate Finance* provides an accessibly-written guide to contemporary financial institutional practice. Professor Rau deploys both his professional expertise and his experience of teaching MBA and graduate-level courses to produce a lively discussion of the key concepts of finance, liberally illustrated with real-world examples. Built around six essential paradigms, he creates an integrated framework covering all the major ideas in finance over the past half-century. Ideal for students and practitioners alike, it will become core reading for anyone aspiring to become an effective manager.

RAGHAVENDRA RAU is the Sir Evelyn de Rothschild Professor of Finance at the University of Cambridge's Judge Business School. He is a director of the Cambridge Centre for Alternative Finance, past president of the European Finance Association, and past editor of the journal *Financial Management*. Professor Rau was Principal at Barclays Global Investors, then the largest asset manager in the world, from 2008 to 2009 and had a ringside view of the financial meltdown. His research has frequently been covered by the popular press, including the *New York Times*, the *Financial Times*, the *Wall Street Journal*, and the *Economist*, among others. He won the Ig Nobel Prize for Management in 2015, a prize awarded for research that makes people laugh, and then think.

Cambridge Short Introductions

Cambridge Short Introductions to Management are short, authoritative, reasonably priced, introductory books for MBA, Masters-level, and executive students taking a management course. Each book is thoroughly class tested and will stand alone as a valuable introduction to a particular subject area, although lecturers may choose to recommend a selection from the series as preparatory reading for a particular course of study. Written by experts from the world's leading business schools, these books are also highly recommended for anyone preparing to study for an advanced Management qualification.

Series Advisors

Richard Barker: Saïd Business School, University of Oxford
Sir Cary L. Cooper CBE: University of Manchester
Thomas G. Cummings: University of Southern California
Marie-Laure Djelic: ESSEC Business School, France
Mauro F. Guillén: Wharton School of Business, University of Pennsylvania
Howard Thomas: Singapore Management University

Titles Published

Barker: *Accounting*
Cascio & Boudreau: *Strategic Human Resource Management*
Andersen: *Strategic Management*

Forthcoming Titles

Nicholson & Coughlan: *Operations Management*
For supplementary materials, visit the series website: www.cambridge.org/csi.

Short Introduction to Corporate Finance

Raghavendra Rau

CAMBRIDGE
UNIVERSITY PRESS

CAMBRIDGE
UNIVERSITY PRESS

University Printing House, Cambridge CB2 8BS, United Kingdom

One Liberty Plaza, 20th Floor, New York, NY 10006, USA

477 Williamstown Road, Port Melbourne, VIC 3207, Australia

314-321, 3rd Floor, Plot 3, Splendor Forum, Jasola District Centre, New Delhi - 110025, India

79 Anson Road, #06-04/06, Singapore 079906

Cambridge University Press is part of the University of Cambridge.

It furthers the University's mission by disseminating knowledge in the pursuit of
education, learning and research at the highest international levels of excellence.

www.cambridge.org
Information on this title: www.cambridge.org/9781107089808
DOI: 10.1017/9781316105795

First published 2017

A catalogue record for this publication is available from the British Library

Library of Congress Cataloging in Publication data
Names: Rau, Raghavendra, 1967– author.
Title: Short introduction to corporate finance / Raghavendra Rau.
Description: New York : Cambridge University Press, [2017] |
Series: Cambridge short introductions to management
Identifiers: LCCN 2016044121 | ISBN 9781107089808 (hardback)
Subjects: LCSH: Corporations – Finance. | Management.
Classification: LCC HG4026 .R37468 2017 | DDC 658.15–dc23
LC record available at https://lccn.loc.gov/2016044121

ISBN 978-1-107-08980-8 Hardback
ISBN 978-1-107-46148-2 Paperback

Additional resources for this publication at www.cambridge.org/csi

Contents

Figures

Tables

Preface

Finance is generally considered one of the most intimidating of the business areas, fit only for extremely quantitative people who are very comfortable with numbers. That belief is rein-forced by the sheer amount of jargon typically used to describe concepts used in finance, such as mortgage-backed securities, mezzanine financing, reverse floaters, inverse repos, quantitative easing, and so on. Thanks to the fact that many people hate mathematics, finance professionals who are comfortable with the numbers successfully parlay the jargon into extremely high, possibly exorbitant[1] salaries. And when the finance firms go too far, taking excessive risks and plunging economies into reces-sions, the popular perception is that the government appears to bail them out, making it a win-win proposition for the bankers and a lose-lose proposition for tax payers.[2]

Do finance professionals deserve the resulting criticism? Or since their jobs are so difficult and complex, do they deserve the salaries they are paid? It turns out that most of finance is really not complex. At its core, finance is composed of a set of just six basic ideas. Five of these six ideas have won their originators Nobel Prizes. Everything in corporate finance can be explained by one or more of these basic ideas.

But what about the jargon? Most of this jargon is just that – jargon. Jargon is extremely useful. It can serve as a shortcut to tell other professionals precisely what a particular type of financial security is. However, with the sheer number of different terms for exactly the same thing[3], a more likely explanation for the explosion in jargon is that it helps completely baffle layper-sons. In fact, to a layperson, the jargon might actually be com-forting. If I want to get my car repaired, the more obscure the terms that the mechanic throws around, the happier I feel that I did not try to fix the car myself (and the more willing I would be to pay that big bill). In finance terms, the more incomprehensible the jargon is, the less willing you are to handle your financial activities yourself, and the more you will be willing to trust a financial advisor who promises to handle the (very necessary[4]) jargon for you. In this book, I am going to shoot myself in the foot by trying to avoid all unnecessary jargon. I will not always succeed in eliminating jargon[5], but I will try to define each technical term as intuitively as I can before using it later.

Despite the bad press which finance has attracted in recent years, these fundamental ideas have not changed. They represent the pinnacle of intellectual achievement in finance, arising from rigorous attempts to understand how to value investments. The emergence of the discipline and practice of corporate finance has fueled innovation and, growth and has significantly improved living standards in the long run.

My hope is that understanding these six seminal ideas at an intuitive level will help you understand the challenge, excitement, and promise of this expanding area of intellectual endeavor, and also expose you to the magic, daily relevance, and fun of the field.

To begin, I will further reduce the six ideas of finance into one basic homespun truth – **there is no free lunch in a competitive market** (or to put it into jargon, arbitrage is not possible in a perfectly competitive market). To put this yet another way, there is only one big idea in finance – no free lunch. No one gives you something for free.

That one big idea forms the basis for understanding everything we know about finance. To see how this is so, we begin in the first chapter by understanding who the major players are in finance and their motivations.

Notes

1. Not according to the finance professionals.
2. See note 1.
3. A simple example would be the yield to maturity for bonds and the internal rate of return for investments, both of which mean the same thing.
4. Or so he says.
5. Sometimes you do need clearly defined shortcuts because otherwise you end up constantly using very convoluted phrases for simple terms. Like calling email a rather cumbersome "courrier électronique" in French, later replaced by the just as rarely used "courriel."

Acknowledgments

I would like to thank Bunny Rau, Kate Belger, Sanjeev Goyal, Andrew Karolyi, Mustafa Leeq, Raghu Rau, Scott Thayer, Naresh Verlander, and, especially, Kathy Kahle and Clive Gallier for detailed comments on early drafts of this manuscript.

1 Who Are the Players in Corporate Finance?

Learning Points

■ The players in corporate finance and their objectives
■ The six ideas in corporate finance

There are four major players in corporate finance – firms, investors, financial intermediaries, and governments.

When we think of firms, we think of big faceless corporate entities that have the right of freedom of speech (in the United States, thanks to the Supreme Court), possibly the right to bear arms[1], and possibly the right to self-defense with lethal force.[2] Yet firms need not be big, nor do they need to have shares that can be purchased on the open market. They do not even have to involve limited liability. In this book, I will refer to firms in the broadest possible sense – they are groups of individuals who work together to achieve a common goal. Your neighborhood coffee shop fits this definition, and so does Microsoft. Firms can have one owner – or a million different shareholders. In the end, they are a collection of individuals working together.

What are the concerns of the firm? They are broadly the same financial concerns that I have as an individual. If I were to think of my two most important financial questions, the first would be how I could make money, and the second would be how I would spend it.[3]

These are the same broad questions firms face. The first question – how the firm spends its money – is called the **investment decision** of the firm. The second – how the firm raises its money – is called the **financing decision** of the firm. *All* decisions that the firm's managers make involve one or the other – the investment or the financing decision. For example, consider a possible human resources decision – the decision of a manager to give her employees a raise. This is an investment decision – the corporation is investing in its human capital. But by choosing to invest in its workers, the firm has less money to invest in something else, say a new machine. In other words, the investment decision does not solely involve physical investment in factories or machines. It involves any kind of investment in any kind of asset that generates benefits for the firm in the future, and it encompasses any area, including marketing, strategy, organizational behavior, or supply chain management.

From whom does the firm raise capital? It can raise capital either directly from individuals or from financial intermediaries who are acting on behalf of the individuals. As an individual, this particular firm is not the only one approaching you. It is one of a huge number of firms, all of which offer different levels of returns for different levels of risk. As an individual, you would like the **highest possible return for the minimum level of risk.**[4] So this is an investment decision for the investor. Of all the firms and of all the contracts offered by each type of firm, which particular contract offers the highest level of return for the minimum risk? The same consideration affects the choice of the financial intermediary to whom you entrust your money, to manage for you. You would like a financial intermediary to find the highest-return, least-risky assets for you. Hopefully, this intermediary will also be the cheapest, but sadly, given the intimidating jargon, many individuals end up paying too much to intermediaries because they associate apparent complexity with quality and quality with costs (and intermediaries have every incentive to overstate the complexity of what they are doing). Severe critics of banks and financial intermediaries argue that having succeeded in preserving the mystique of their art through obfuscation, these institutions then proceed to charge you handsomely for the privilege of embracing their services. In fact, it is not quite that simple. The institutions and some of their employees are not always one-dimensional villains. The functions they perform are very important time-saving alternatives to the monitoring, search, and even higher financing costs that individuals and firms might otherwise face.

What specifically do financial intermediaries do that is so important? One of their major roles is to act as a broker.[5] They bring together providers of finance (the investors) with the organizations that need finance (the firms). They charge for providing this matching service. They also advise firms and managers as to the right price or value of assets and the amount to pay. Financial intermediaries can act on behalf of either the investors or the firms (or both). Examples of intermediaries acting on behalf of the investors include mutual and hedge funds. These collect money from investors and promise to invest the money in assets that provide the highest return for the minimum amount of risk. They make money by charging fees for the investment service. Another intermediary is a commercial bank. The bank aggregates deposits from individuals and lends the aggregated deposits to firms in the form of loans. It makes money by charging an interest rate to borrowers that is higher than the rate it pays to the individuals depositing money with the bank. It can also make profits (which can be very significant) by managing the relative maturities of the loans it makes and the deposits it takes according to the pattern of interest rates over different time horizons (what is called the term structure of interest rates). An investment bank is yet another type of intermediary that advises the firm on raising capital, buying other firms (acquisitions), and other corporate activities. It makes money by charging the firms substantial fees for these services.

Finally, governments form the last set of players in the financial markets. The government typically has three effects on the economy. First, it plays a reallocation role. It takes money away from one sector and gives it to another. Sometimes this is efficient, in that the sectors to which resources are being allocated are more productive than sectors from which resources are being taken away. Sometimes this is because sectors that complain loudly are given large allocations, while sectors that do not complain have money taken away, which is not necessarily efficient. An example of the latter is subsidies. Subsidies typically help one narrow sector of the economy. However, they hurt other sectors that pay taxes but do not receive subsidies. Mortgage tax relief is a subsidy that helps home owners at the expense of renters. A tax on sugar imports hurts the general sugar consuming population to benefit a narrow group of sugar growers. The taxes and subsidies set by the government also play important roles in corporate finance and individual financial decisions. For example, the various rates that form the tax schedule faced by individuals and firms are central to the firm's assessment of the viability of an investment/project. Similarly, because interest on debt is tax deductible while dividends paid to shareholders are not, this has significant implications for how firms choose to finance themselves. The government's responsibility for managing fluctuations in the local currency and its exchange rates also has implications for firms and individuals, particularly those involved in international trade with cash flows denominated in a foreign currency. The inflation rate, which the government (either directly or through a central bank) attempts to control and manage, is key to the real and nominal interest rate structure that features in investing and financing decisions.

Second, the government has a multiplier effect. In a recession, some economists argue that the government should increase the demand for products and services by enacting policies that increase demand. For example, governments should spend money on roads and even, according to theory, on digging holes. Workers will then go out and spend their pay, providing further cash to businesses, who will then hire more workers, spend the money on wages, and so on. Preferably, the government investment should not crowd out possible private investment that firms would have done by themselves anyway. This use of taxes and spending to move the economy – that is, fiscal policy or demand management – was central to the policy prescriptions of John Maynard Keynes in the late 1930s. When there is a gap between a government's expenditure and its revenues, it bridges that gap by borrowing or raising debt, which involves the government setting a price in its bid for funds to cover the funding gap. This too has implications for the theory and practice of corporate finance. Most governments retain sovereignty and responsibility for economic growth (measured by GDP per capita), and for measures allied to productivity, the level of unemployment, the health and state of its international accounts with other nations, that is, its balance of payments, and finally the level of general price inflation. These government activities – while in essence the subject of a macroeconomics course and therefore beyond the scope of this book – influence variables that loom very large in the investing and financing

decisions of firms and individuals. For example, we will see
in the upcoming chapters that the risk-free rate is a crucial
variable for the financing and investing decisions made by both
firms and investors. This variable is the rate bid for government
benchmark debt, which can be short-term or longer (five, ten, or
even thirty years). This is in turn dependent on the government's
budgetary position. The risk-free rate is central to the
computation of the discount rate (through a capital-asset pricing
model defined later in this chapter), which in turn is essential for
deciding the firm's investment policy.

Finally, the government plays a regulatory role. It tells
investors and firms what they can or cannot do. Governments
play an active role in shaping the regulatory environment for
business. Firms and individuals factor the relevant details of the
current environment into their financing and investing decisions.

All these different players and their interactions can be
summed up in Figure 1.1.

These different players appear to have multiple possibly
conflicting objectives. However, their decisions are still governed
by the same basic six ideas I mention above. What are these six
ideas?

The Six Ideas of Corporate Finance

Net Present Value (NPV): The first idea is that of Net Present
Value (NPV). Consider the investment decision of the firm. The
investment decision involves payoffs. The basic idea is that
managers aim to maximize the Net Present Value of all these
payoffs from any decision, and the decision rule is that the
manager needs to invest if and only if the net present value
of the investment is positive. There are only three steps in
computing NPV. The first step is computing all the cash flows
from a particular investment. Unfortunately, although some of
these cash flows arise right away, others may arise several years
later (the initial investment usually happens today and payoffs
occur in the future). Hence, the second step is to compute the
value of all these payoffs at one point of time. This involves
computing the discount rate. This is an interest rate that tells

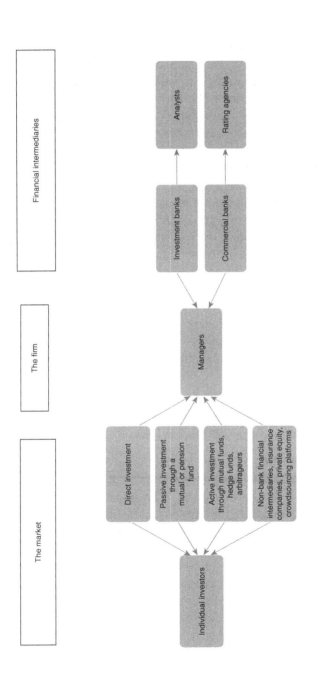

Figure 1.1 The players and their interactions

you the value today of a payoff you will get sometime in the future. By using the discount rate, we can collapse all future cash flows into one current value, which can then be netted against the initial cost. The third and final step involves deciding how to finance the asset. The major reason this is important is taxes. Some forms of financing (debt for example) are tax-deductible – interest is paid before taxes are paid, thus reducing taxes. So the after-tax cost of debt is reduced. Hence, the mix of financing changes the effective interest rate you pay.

Portfolio Theory and the Capital Asset Pricing Model: Computing the NPV involves calculating the interest rate. Where does this rate come from? Investors decide this interest rate, not the firm. Recall that the firm is approaching the investor to raise financing. But the firm is only one of several who are simultaneously approaching the investor. In other words, the investor needs to decide how to allocate her savings among all the investment opportunities she is faced with. In order to invest in a particular firm, the firm needs to offer a rate of return at least as good as the next-best alternative the investor has. But how do we find the next-best alternative for every investor? The answer to this conundrum was proposed by Harry Markowitz and Bill Sharpe, who were awarded the 1990 Nobel Prize in Economics[6] for their contribution. The essence of their contribution was to note that individuals do not actually hold investments in isolation. They hold them as parts of an investment portfolio. The investment portfolio has both an expected return and a level of risk, which can be computed statistically if we know what the level of risk and return are for the individual investments in the portfolio. If we then combine the investment portfolio with a riskless asset such as a government bond, we can identify a unique portfolio – the market portfolio – the return to which determines the discount rate for any investment. The actual formula they came up with to calculate the discount rate is called the Capital Asset Pricing Model formula or the CAPM (pronounced CAP-M) for short.

Capital Structure Theory: Capital structure theory defines how the discount rate is affected by the forms of capital the firm chooses to raise, typically debt or equity. Knowing what different types of investors demand in the form of returns, enables the firm to plan its amount and type of financing. All types of financing are not equivalent. Specifically, interest on debt is usually tax-deductible while dividends (returns obtained from equity) are usually not. Should the firm issue debt or equity? Franco Modigliani and Merton Miller both received a Nobel Prize for answering this question systematically.[7] The idea is that in a perfect world (there are no taxes, everyone has the same level of information, and there are no lawyers (no bankruptcy costs)), the form of financing does not matter. As they show in a proof that is directly taken from the no-free-lunch idea, the value of the firm is unaffected by whether you choose to finance the firm's investment by equity, debt, or the earnings generated by the firm. However, once you start letting in imperfections, such as taxes, asymmetric information, and so on, the form of financing does matter.

Option Pricing Theory: A range of investment decisions that the firm makes (the decision to start a new factory, for example) cannot be analyzed easily using NPV. To understand these decisions, we need option pricing theory. A call option gives you the right to buy a particular asset at a price we fix today. But – and this is the key ingredient of an option – we are not obliged to go through with the deal. If the market price of the asset falls, for example, we will no longer want to carry out the deal (since we can buy it cheaper on the open market), and thanks to the option, we don't have to. Similarly, buying a put option gives us the right to sell the asset at a price we fix today. However, it is important to note that the seller of the option does not have the right to refuse you when you wish to buy or sell. For example, when the buyer wishes to exercise a call option, the seller must turn over the asset and take the fixed price in exchange. This will inevitably happen only when the deal is unfavorable to the option seller (the asset must be worth more than the fixed price, or the option holder will not exercise). To persuade the option seller to sell the option, he has to charge a price up front. Option pricing theory tells you what that price should be. Too high a price means that no one will buy the option from you. Setting too low a price on a regular basis means that when the buyers exercise the options, you will eventually be bankrupted.

How should the option seller set the price? The answer to this question was provided by Fischer Black, Myron Scholes, and Robert Merton, the latter two of whom shared the 1997 Nobel Prize in Economics for their solution.[8] Their answer was also a direct application of the no-free-lunch idea. They set up a portfolio that consisted of the underlying asset and a riskless asset, a bond, that had the same final payoff as the option. The no-free-lunch principle says that if two assets have the same final payoff, they must have the same initial cost. Hence, since we can compute the cost of a portfolio of the asset and the bond that perfectly replicates the payoff to the option, the cost of the portfolio must be the cost of the option.

Asymmetric Information: Every transaction you make involves asymmetric information. Suppose you are trying to buy a used car. The seller of the car is likely to have much more information than you on the true value of the car, whether the car is in good condition, whether the seller has skimped on servicing and maintenance, and so on. The seller always has the incentive to claim to you that the car is in amazingly good condition. Does this mean that you are worse off? Interestingly enough, the answer is no. You know you are informationally disadvantaged. Hence, you will drop your buying price to take the disadvantage into account. The sellers who are selling very good cars are disadvantaged (because you offer just the average price) and have incentives to prove that the car is in really good condition. This idea is one of the most influential ideas in financial economics, and can be used to understand everything from the used car market to executive pay scandals, business ethics, and financial policy. George Akerlof, Michael Spence, and Joseph Stiglitz shared the 2001 Nobel Prize for developing some seminal ideas in analyzing markets with asymmetric information.

Market Efficiency: Efficient markets are markets that fully reflect all available information. While this seems like a simple idea, this is possibly the most controversial one in corporate finance. The problem is that market efficiency does not tell us the relationship between market prices and the fundamental NPV of the asset. As noted above, computing the NPV involves computing the cash flows, the discount rate, and adjusting the discount rate for the financing structure of the firm. Now suppose economists use the CAPM to compute the discount rate but investors do not (they use a different asset pricing model). Prices will change when new information arrives but not in a way the economist believes they will. Does this mean that markets are not efficient? Are investors not behaving rationally, or are the economists using the wrong model? In addition, investors have a range of systematic behavioral biases, and we are unable to predict which bias dominates and when the biases shift in importance. Regardless, three economists – Daniel Kahneman (2002), Eugene Fama (2013), and Robert Shiller (2013) all received Nobel Prizes for pioneering ideas that influenced this field.

So there we have it. Six ideas, five of which have been cited in awarded Nobels, govern the entirety of corporate finance. And all of them are derived from the no-arbitrage or no-free-lunch idea. Let's relate all this to the big picture. The figure below shows cash flows between firms and investors and goes on to show where the six big ideas fit in.

On the left-hand side of the figure lie the investors (the market). They are offered a menu of contracts by the firm on the right-hand side. Some of these contracts involve fixed payments every year or every six months, a promise to return the face value at the end of a fixed term, and a promise to pay off the instrument holders first in case of default. These contracts are debt contracts. Similarly, another set of contracts offers no guarantee of payments and the possibility of being paid last, if at all, if the firm defaults on its other contracts and goes bankrupt. Why would someone buy such a contract? Because it offers a possibility of large payments if the firm succeeds. To put this another way, it offers an opportunity to invest in the growth potential of the firm. We call these contracts equity. Other contracts (preferred shares, convertible bonds, and so on) may also exist. Investors decide what these contracts are worth based on what they are already holding (their portfolios) and how risky these contracts are (the Capital Asset Pricing Model). That sets the price for these contracts, what we call the bond price (for debt) and the share price (for equity).

The investors buy the share and bond contracts and transfer the money to the firm. The firm then chooses to invest

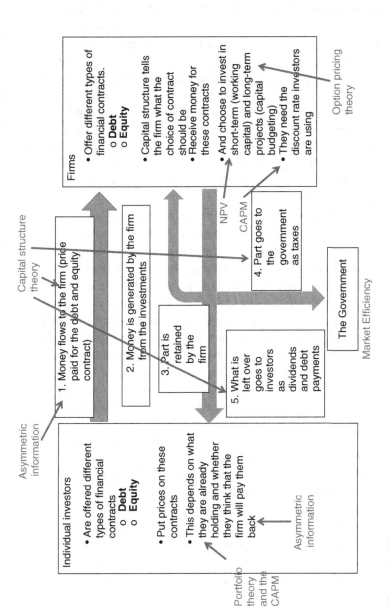

Figure 1.2 Where do the six ideas fit in?

Individual investors

- Are offered different types of financial contracts
  - Debt
  - Equity
- Put prices on these contracts
- This depends on what they are already holding and whether they think that the firm will pay them back

Asymmetric information

Portfolio theory and the CAPM

1. Money flows to the firm (price paid for the debt and equity contract)

2. Money is generated by the firm from the investments

3. Part is retained by the firm

4. Part goes to the government as taxes

5. What is left over goes to investors as dividends and debt payments

The Government

Market Efficiency

Capital structure theory

Asymmetric information

Firms

- Offer different types of financial contracts.
  - Debt
  - Equity
- Capital structure tells the firm what the choice of contract should be
- Receive money for these contracts
- And choose to invest in short-term (working capital) and long-term projects (capital budgeting)
- They need the discount rate investors are using

Option pricing theory

NPV

CAPM

these inflows into either short-term (current) assets or long-term assets using NPV as its decision rule. It chooses projects to maximize the NPV. To compute the NPV, it needs the discount rate, which it obtains from the prices that investors have paid for the shares and bonds. The discount rate is affected by the capital structure – the mixture of stocks and bonds the firm has issued. This mix also affects the taxes the firm pays, the amount of debt and dividend payments it makes, and the earnings it retains for further investment. Some of the firm's decisions cannot be analyzed with simple NPV tools. For example, strategic learning involves real options, as does the option to expand or abandon a project. To value these, the firm needs option theory.

Finally, the amount the investors pay for contracts is also affected by asymmetric information. The firm's managers have greater information on the true value of the firm's assets than outside investors. Like used car salesmen, they have incentives to claim the assets are worth a fortune when they may be useless. Investors take this into account when pricing the security contracts. Firms design managerial incentives and other mechanisms (collectively titled "corporate governance mechanisms") to alter the level of asymmetric information and hence the prices that investors are willing to pay.

And underlying everything else lies the idea of market efficiency. If markets cannot somehow compute the fundamental value of any asset and relate it to prices, then the rest of finance theory falls apart. It is not much use estimating the fundamental value of an asset using NPV, portfolio theory, and capital structure theory, if market prices are not even in the same ballpark as the value you have calculated. Is the market wrong? Suppose the market is wrong and the firm is deeply valuable while the market thinks the firm is of no value. Would you be correct in buying the shares of this firm? If the market never realizes the value of the firm before the time comes for you to liquidate your shares, the shares will always be largely worthless to you. Hence, your investment will never pay off in your lifetime, and you will be largely left holding worthless scraps of paper.[9] Hence, for the six finance ideas to be valuable, markets must sooner or later relate fundamental values (computed according to the six ideas) to the market prices. To put it another way, if the market is using a completely different method of valuation that is not in the six ideas of corporate finance, financial economists might as well pack up their bags and go home.

Notes

1. Giving a whole new meaning to the term "corporate warfare."
2. The last two rights have not yet been granted to corporations by the U.S. Supreme Court as of the time of writing.
3. Note that if we apply finance theory properly, we do not actually need to make the money *before* we spend it.
4. Feel free to contact me personally if you would like an investment opportunity that offers the highest possible risk for the minimum level of return.
5. Similar to a real estate or a marriage broker.
6. Strictly speaking, it is called the Sveriges Riksbank Prize in Economic Sciences in Memory of Alfred Nobel. Since that is a little unwieldy, I'm going to refer to this as the Nobel Prize in Economics.
7. Though in separate years (1985 and 1990 respectively), and not quite for the same contribution. The Nobel Prize committee cited Franco Modigliani's life-cycle hypothesis as the basis for his prize. However, the life-cycle hypothesis is also proved in a similar way. We have a limited number of ideas in finance and an even more limited number of ways to prove something.
8. Fischer Black was dead by then, and the Nobel Prize is not awarded posthumously.
9. These scraps might be valuable as cattle feed, though possibly not as human nourishment.

2 NPV and the Investment Decision of the Firm

Learning Points

- What is the goal of a firm's managers? To maximize shareholder value?
- Stakeholders vs. shareholders: Why do we focus only on maximizing the value to shareholders?
- NPV: Which shareholders' value do we maximize? Long-term vs. short-term shareholders?
- Deriving the NPV rule
- The different types of cash flows used in the NPV rule

To understand why NPV is so important, let us start with two very simple questions. What is the goal of the firm's managers? In whose interests should the firm be run?

Stakeholders vs. Shareholders

Let's start by listing the different stakeholders in the firm in Figure 2.1.

These stakeholders represent everyone who has a stake in the success of the firm. Obvious examples are the workers, the managers, the shareholders, the customers, the suppliers, the bondholders, regulators, auditors, and so on. Some examples are not quite so obvious. For example, competitors also have a (negative) stake in the firm. A firm succeeding means that its competitors might be worse off. Competitors have incentives to complain that their rivals are pricing their products too low, bundling different services into a package to hide underlying costs, or engaging in any other activity that leaves the competitors worse off. The government also has a stake in the firm – if the firm fails, its employees will be out of jobs with the corresponding unemployment benefits being picked up by the

Figure 2.1 The different stakeholders in the firm

taxpayers. If the firm is too successful, the government worries that these profits are at the expense of other competitors or workers.

The managers are the ones in charge of the firm's investment and financing policies. With all these different stakeholders, which ones should they satisfy? Interestingly, the answer to this question varies by country. In developed countries, the United States and the United Kingdom are among the only ones where managers prioritize shareholders. In most of the other developed markets in which these surveys have been conducted, including France, Germany, and Japan, managers say that all stakeholders are important.[1]

If you ask American or British academics, they will all say that the firm should be run in the interests of the shareholders. No one else appears to get a look in. And this attitude appears to be reflected in the attitudes of their respective country managers.[2]

Why is shareholder value important? The typical answer given by managers is that shareholders are the owners of the firm. They provide capital to the firm and hence they should benefit. But this is not as obvious as you might think. Yes, the shareholders provide capital. But it is a particular type of capital – financial capital. The bondholders also provide a different type of financial capital (debt capital). Workers do not provide financial capital but provide human capital. The entrepreneur who originally set up the firm provides the idea – the intellectual capital. Why should one type of (financial) capital be more important than all these other types of capital? Wouldn't it be better to maximize the value of all stakeholders, not just shareholders but everyone else as well?

Let's start by thinking about this conceptually. Suppose you were asked to organize an office party and pick a particular restaurant that makes everyone happy. You know that none of the other office workers are very social[3], and so once the venue is picked, none of them will talk to each other about their preferences. If this is the case, the decision is very easy for you. Pick a restaurant that you like. If anyone complains, saying that they would have preferred another restaurant, just say that this was the choice that made everyone else happy. Translating to firmspeak, the manager knows that the different stakeholders will not coordinate with each other as to what makes them happy. So the manager chooses to make himself happy, spending on perks[4] and anything else that benefits the manager personally. The moral is simple: Giving the manager a job description that says make everyone happy is a fool's errand. No one can do this. A manager with this objective will be the only one who is happy.

So we need to pick one particular stakeholder and make that stakeholder happy while optimizing the value of everyone else. Finance theory tells you that the stakeholder you pick is the shareholder.

So what makes shareholders the privileged ones? Why should the firm be managed only in their interests? What about the other stakeholders? Will they get ignored or worse, hurt or killed even, if firms pursue shareholder value ahead of everything else? For example, consider Apple, which produces and assembles most of the components in its products via subcontractors in China. In 2010, workers at an Apple assembler in eastern China were injured when they were ordered by the supplier managers to clean iPhone screens using a poisonous chemical.[5] Similar conditions were documented at other firms such as Dell, IBM, Lenovo, and others. Several Foxconn workers in Shenzhen, China, the site of another supplier of iPad components, apparently attempted to commit

suicide as a result of the harsh working conditions including
the pressure imposed on them by their managers. Similarly,
in 2013, a building housing five garment factories in Dhaka,
Bangladesh, collapsed killing more than a thousand workers.[6] A
government report concluded that the building was constructed
with substandard materials, revealing a blatant disregard for
statutory building codes. Despite knowing that the building
was unsafe, the managers of the factories, apparently fixated
on profits, urged their workers to keep working. How do we
reconcile stories like this with our emphasis that shareholder
value maximization is the only correct goal for managers?

There are several distinctions to make here. First, and most
important, profit maximization is *not* the same as shareholder
value maximization. A fixation on profits may indeed make
managers ill-treat some stakeholders at the cost of everyone
else. But this could ultimately lead to a destruction of
shareholder value. For example, if managers treat workers badly,
the workers will produce shoddy products, which will affect
profits and then the share price. The point is that share prices
are the present values of *all* profits to be received at any time
in the future. Maximizing next year's profits by treating workers
badly may reduce profits five years from now. Bad publicity will
affect the demand for the firm's products and that will also
affect the share price. The key is that shareholders are paid
after everyone else. So maximizing the value of shareholders
automatically means optimizing the value of other stakeholders.

As an example, in 1991, Nike was targeted by anti–sweat
shop campaigners who organized a global boycott of its products
after evidence emerged that Nike's subcontractors (in the Asian
subcontinent and in Southeast Asia) were using child labor to
manufacture its products.[7] Nike responded with a factory code
of conduct. After protests at the Barcelona Olympics in 1992
and mainstream media attention, Nike established a department
to improve the lives of factory laborers. After further unrest that
spread to college students protesting against the company in
1997, Nike CEO, Phil Knight, announced in May 1998 that Nike
would raise the minimum age of workers, increase monitoring
at its subcontractors, and adopt U.S. clean air standards in all
its factories. Over the next few years, it performed an increasing

number of factory audits and published a complete list of all the factories it contracted with. While Nike still is criticized on occasion, its image has improved markedly.[8]

So the first reason we focus on shareholder value is because it is a clear simple goal. It focuses on one number. That number is of critical importance to shareholders who are paid after everyone else.

But it seems unfair that we are just satisficing everyone else while maximizing the value for shareholders. To answer this issue, the key to remember is that the other stakeholders have explicit contracts with the firm. For example, a worker will work for a firm under an explicit contract that specifies the salary, possible bonuses, severance pay, holiday leave, and so on. If the worker puts in the effort, but the firm violates the explicit contract by not paying the worker, giving someone else the bonus, and so on, the worker can (and usually will) sue the firm in a court of law. Similarly, a bondholder has an explicit contract with the firm on the terms of debt repayment, the interest paid, any covenants governing actions the firm can take, and so on. If the firm violates any of these terms (it does not make an interest payment on time, for example), it usually goes into bankruptcy, and the bondholders take over the firm. A customer's explicit contract covers the right to return the product in case of defects, the quality of the product, and so on. Customers have the ability to sue the firm if these terms are violated. Similar types of contracts govern the interactions between the firm and all its stakeholders. The only stakeholder who is not covered by an explicit contract is the shareholder. The shareholder has the right to vote at annual meetings (and in many of these cases, the votes are nonbinding) but no right to annual dividends (which are given at the discretion of the firm's managers). So the shareholder is almost the only stakeholder who is not protected explicitly by the law. Essentially, this means that, of all the stakeholders, the shareholder will be the most nervous about giving any capital to the firm.

So the second reason we focus on shareholder value as the primary goal for managers is the lack of explicit protection for them.

It is important to note that focusing on shareholder value will not solve all issues. Apple for example, was criticized for harsh working practices among its supplier workers as far ago as 2006.[9] In response, Apple ordered annual audit reports on its direct suppliers and many of its suppliers' suppliers. Despite these audits, problems persist, as shown by the more recent news articles detailed above. However, Apple remains one of the most admired brands in the United States. In a 2011 *New York Times* survey, 56% of respondents said that they could not think of anything negative about Apple. Until consumers demand better conditions at supplier factories and vote with their wallets, Apple has no incentive to radically improve working conditions in its supply chain. To put this another way, if the shareholders (and indirectly customers or other members of society) do not care about an issue, the firm will not change its behavior. Does this suggest a role for government? I will defer this issue and other issues of social responsibility to Chapter 6, on corporate governance and asymmetric information. Chapter 6 also addresses the issue of how firm managers can convince shareholders that their capital will not simply be stolen by the managers. In this chapter, I will assume that firm managers are honest and hard-working and *want* to maximize shareholder value (which, as I note above, automatically assumes optimization of other stakeholders' values).

Which Shareholder Is More Important? Long-Term vs. Short-Term Shareholders

However, maximizing shareholder value is also a more complicated concept than it appears. Different shareholders have different investment horizons. Suppose the firm has a choice between a long-term project and a short-term project. The long-term project pays off in fifty years and returns no cash flows before then. The short-term project returns cash flows two years from now, and then the firm has to find a different short-term project to invest in. Now suppose that there are two types of investors – a set of ninety-year-old retirees and a bunch of twenty-five-year old recent MBA graduates. Which project should the firm take?

One possible answer is to satisfy the majority. But a typical manager does not even know who *any* of her shareholders are, let alone if the majority are short-term or long-term. And even if she does know the identity of some institutional shareholders, it is unclear which of these shareholders is more important. For example, consider the manager of a Japanese firm with a number of long-term Japanese shareholders and a couple of short-term activist American large institutional shareholders. Which ones should the manager satisfy?

To get a more formal sense of the problem, we need to introduce a few graphs here. Let's start with an extremely simple world – a desert island where two survivors from a shipwreck, Saruman and Galadriel, have been washed ashore. They are completely cut off from the outside world, no communications, and no Internet access. They have been washed ashore with a bag of potatoes, which they proceed to divide equally among themselves. For example, if the bag were to contain 100 potatoes, they would get 50 each.[10]

Each of them has to choose how many of their 50 potatoes to plant (to harvest next season) and how many to consume this season. Saruman and Galadriel divide the island into two (with equal-size areas of identical fertility, soil quality, sunlight, water, and other production relevant factors). Each chooses one area to plant his or her potatoes within their respective plots. Now potatoes, like many commodities, exhibit declining returns to scale. Saruman and Galadriel will logically plant potatoes in the most fertile areas first. The next set will be planted in less fertile areas and so on, till the potatoes run out. This means that doubling the amount of potatoes planted will not double the output next period. If four potatoes are planted, Saruman and Galadriel will get back, say, six each. However, if eight potatoes are planted, they will not get back twelve, but say ten each. Figure 2.2 shows how declining returns to scale can be modeled.

In this figure, the X-axis is the number of potatoes this season (season 0) (P_0), and the Y-axis represents the number of potatoes next season (season 1) (P_1). Now the initial endowment of potatoes for each of Saruman and Galadriel is 50.

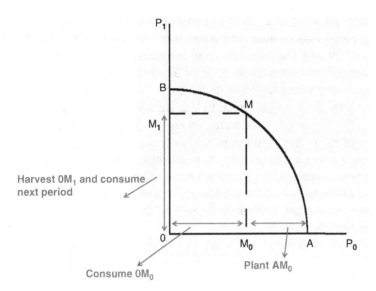

Figure 2.2 The production function for potatoes

This is represented by the point A on the X-axis. In period 0, Saruman and Galadriel each make the choice how much to plant (invest) and how much to consume. Suppose they pick M_0 as their optimal point. Then M_0A represents how many potatoes are planted. The remaining distance $0M_0$ represents how many potatoes they consume this season. Next season, they harvest $0M_1$ and consume it all.[11]

Let's now think about how to model the choice of Saruman and Galadriel on how much to consume this season and how much to plant (the choice of the point M_0 on the X-axis). Economists like to model this choice using what are called preference curves (sometimes called indifference curves).[12] To understand what indifference curves are, consider going to the supermarket. You pile a bunch of groceries into your basket. Now there are lots of combinations you would be indifferent between. For example, suppose an economist were to offer you the following two basket options: Basket 1 (one pizza, eight tomatoes, and two onions) or Basket 2 (one pizza, six tomatoes, and three onions). The baskets are the same price. You might shrug your shoulders if the economist were to ask you to choose between them. In economist parlance, you would be indifferent between these choices. However, if the economist were then to offer Basket 3 which consists of *two* pizzas, *ten* tomatoes, and *four* onions for the same price as Baskets 1 and 2, any rational consumer would definitely prefer Basket 3 to either 1 or 2 – rational people prefer more to less (for the same outlay).

But if you really like pizza, asking you to give up the pizza in return for getting more tomatoes or more onions (for the same price) would be a big deal. You might demand twenty more tomatoes to give up even one slice of pizza. Or you might be willing to give up all the tomatoes and all the onions for an additional pizza. All these preferences can be represented by preference curves.

Figure 2.3 shows a pair of preference curves. As before, the X-axis is the number of potatoes this season (P_0), and the Y-axis represents the number of potatoes next season (P_1). On any individual preference curve itself, the consumer is indifferent between every combination of potatoes this and next season. For example, point Y on the lower curve AA is a combination of a larger amount of potatoes this season (Y_0) and fewer potatoes next season (Y_1). Point X involves giving up some potatoes today (X_0 is smaller than Y_0) and getting a few more potatoes

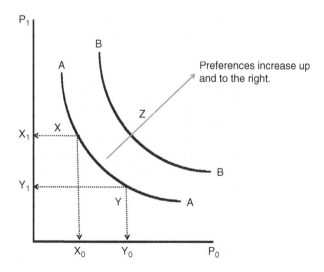

Figure 2.3 Preference curves

next season (X_1 is larger than Y_1). Since they are on the same preference curve, however, the consumer is indifferent between the two points. Point Z is on a higher indifference curve BB. The idea is that people will always prefer more to less, so given a choice between (1) ten potatoes this season and fifteen next season and (2) twelve potatoes this season and sixteen next season, every rational person will prefer option 2 to option 1. Point Z is preferred to point X because you get more potatoes today *and* the same number of potatoes next season. Point Z is preferred to point Y because you get the same number of potatoes this season *but* a higher number of potatoes next season.

The slope of the preference curve tells you how impatient the person is. An impatient person (who wants immediate gratification) is very reluctant to give up current consumption for some nebulous future consumption. To tempt the person into giving up even a few potatoes today, you have to offer him a large number of potatoes tomorrow. Or equivalently, the person would be willing to give up a large number of potatoes tomorrow to get just a few more potatoes today. This would be a very steep preference curve represented by the lower steep curve CC in Figure 2.4. Similarly, the shallow preference curve

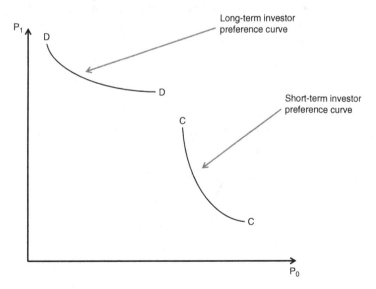

Figure 2.4 Short-term and long-term investor preference curves

DD represents a long-term individual who cares about long-term payoffs, not today's consumption. So to persuade her to give up any potatoes next season, you would have to offer her a large number of potatoes today.

Now let us suppose that Saruman is a short-term investor. He only cares about this season and not so much about the next.[13] Galadriel is the exact opposite – she cares a lot about next season and not so much about this season. She is a long-term investor. What will their consumption and planting decisions look like? All we need to do is superimpose their preference curves onto the production function for potatoes. Figure 2.5 shows Saruman's optimal investment and consumption decisions.

Saruman chooses to plant very little today. Specifically, he chooses to plant S_0A, and consume the rest, OS_0. Why the particular point S? There are a number of other preference curves available (modeled by M and M_1 in the graph). However, Saruman will continue going rightward till the preference curve is tangent to the production function at only one point, the point S. This is the maximum he can get, given the production function. The function also shows that he will harvest OS_1 next season and consume it right away (recall that they are rescued at the end of season 2, so they do not need to plant anything in this season; there is no season 3).

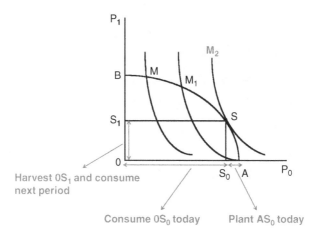

Figure 2.5 Saruman's optimal investment and consumption decision

Galadriel, in contrast, is a long-term investor. She chooses to consume very little today. Specifically, she chooses to plant G_0A, and consume the rest, $0G_0$. From the production function, she will harvest $0G_1$ next season and consume that right away. Figure 2.6 models her optimal investment and consumption decision.

The problem occurs when both Saruman and Galadriel decide to work together. What will be the optimal amount they will choose to plant and to consume? They can never come to a decision that will make them both happy. G is to the left of S, so any point between G and S will make Saruman unhappier than picking S alone. Similarly, S is below G, so any point between S and G will make Galadriel unhappier than picking G alone. Unfortunately, this means that the two will never be able to come to an agreement that leaves them both better off than before by pooling their endowments.

Now let us introduce a third castaway, Mr. Banks. Robin (as Mr. Banks is known to his friends) decides to start a potato exchange. He offers a constant interest rate, r. If you borrowed 1 potato from him, you would have to return $1 + r$ potatoes next season. The interest rate line is flat, however, and so if you lent him a potato, he would return $1 + r$ next season. Putting

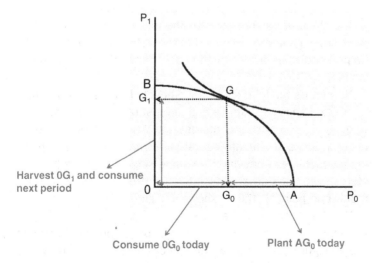

Figure 2.6 Galadriel's optimal investment and consumption decision

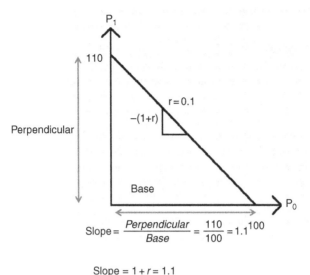

Figure 2.7 The interest rate line

numbers on this, if the interest rate were 10%, you would get back 11 potatoes if you lent Robin 10 potatoes, 22 if you lent him 20 and so on. Similarly, if you borrowed 50 potatoes, you would have to return 55 and so on. The interest rate line is depicted in Figure 2.7 for an interest rate of 10%.

The slope of the interest rate line tells us the interest rate. High school geometry tells us that the definition of the slope is the perpendicular divided by the base, hence the slope of the line is equal to $1 + r$.

Now let us model the optimal production decision given the potato exchange's existence and interest rate. To do this, all we do is superimpose the interest rate line on the production function. Since all the interest rate lines are perfectly straight and parallel lines (they have the same slope), we move the interest rate line outwards till it touches the production function at only one point N. This is shown in Figure 2.8.

Now let us see what happens to Saruman. His original optimal point was S in Figure 2.5. We now propose to bring him to S' in Figure 2.9. Saruman would obviously prefer S' to S – he gets much more today for only a small amount less tomorrow.

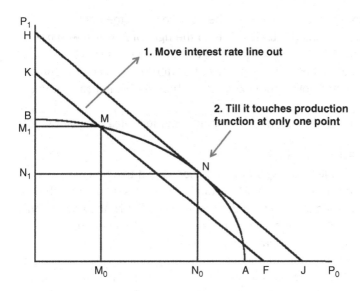

Figure 2.8 Optimal production decision with the interest rate line

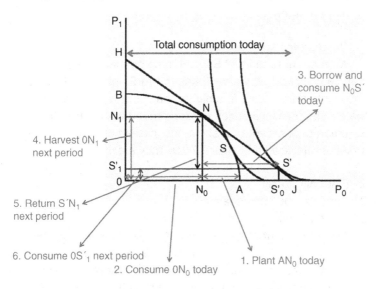

Figure 2.9 Saruman's optimal investment and consumption decision with borrowing

In preference curve terms, he has moved to the right. But how does he get there? S′ is to the right of A, which was his original endowment. In other words, if he originally was given 50 potatoes, he is proposing to eat 55 today and *still* have some left over to plant for next season. That seems impossible but it is not.

To get Saruman to S′, consider the following series of steps:

1. Plant AN_0 today.
2. This leaves ON_0 that can be consumed this season.
3. The investment of AN_0 returns ON_1 next season from the production function. But before the point N, the production function is steeper than the interest rate line (it offers a better return than the potato exchange).
4. Since Saruman only wants to consume OS'_1 next season, he offers to return the difference S'_1N_1 to Robin next season.
5. Robin is working with the interest rate line and offers to lend Saruman N_0S' today in return for getting back S'_1N_1 next season (the interest rate line is less steep than the production function). Saruman therefore can now consume $ON_0 + N_0S' = OS'$ this season and OS'_1 next season, leaving him better off.

These steps are illustrated in Figure 2.9.

What about Galadriel? She can also be made better off. Her original point was G. We can bring her to G′ in Figure 2.10, which she would prefer since it is higher than G. How does she get there? She follows a series of steps that are similar to the ones Saruman took except that she lends instead of borrowing. Her steps are illustrated in Figure 2.10. They are:

1. Plant AN_0 today.
2. Consume OG'_0 this season.
3. The remainder G'_0N_0 is lent to Robin.
4. The investment of AN_0 returns ON_1 next season from the production function. After the point N, the interest rate line is steeper than the production function (it offers a better return than planting the potatoes in the ground).
5. Robin returns G'_1N_1 to Galadriel next season.

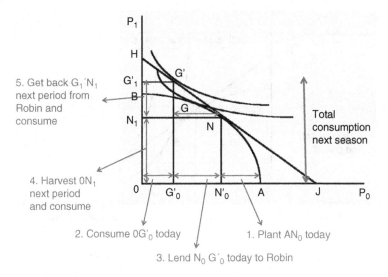

Figure 2.10 Galadriel's optimal investment and consumption decision with lending

6. Galadriel can therefore now consume $ON_1 + N_1G'_1 = OG'_1$ next season and OG'_0 this season, leaving her better off as well.

Part of Saruman's and Galadriel's strategies are common sense. The production function and the interest rate line have different slopes. Hence, it makes sense to borrow at the cheapest rate and invest at the highest rate. If the interest rate line is less steep than the production function, it makes sense for Saruman to borrow from Robin (at a lower interest rate) rather than cut back on his investment (which is on the production function). If the interest rate line is steeper than the production function, it also makes sense for Galadriel to lend to Robin (at a higher interest rate) instead of investing in the production function. The key though is that step 1, which determines the optimal investment amount, is exactly the same for Galadriel and Saruman (step 1 is the same for both of them).

Let us take this to an extreme. Suppose Saruman wants absolutely nothing next period. What is the maximum amount he can borrow today so that he is left with nothing tomorrow after paying off his debt to Robin? This is illustrated in Figure 2.11.

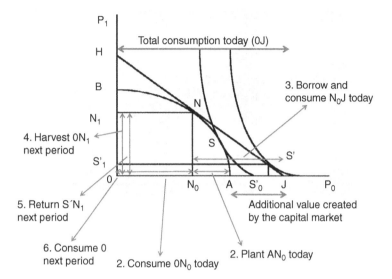

Figure 2.11 Saruman's optimal investment and consumption decision with nothing left over for next season

The steps are:

1. Plant AN_0 today.
2. This leaves ON_0 that can be consumed this season.
3. The investment of AN_0 returns ON_1 next season from the production function.
4. Since Saruman wants to consume 0 next season, he offers to return it all to Robin next season.
5. Robin offers to lend Saruman $N_0 J$ today in return for getting back ON_1 next season. Saruman therefore can now consume $ON_0 + N_0 J = OJ$ this season and 0 next season.

There are two interesting points here: the distance AJ and the point N. Saruman's previous endowment was OA. Now he can go beyond his initial endowment all the way to J. The distance AJ is therefore additional value created by Robin. Without the ability to borrow and lend, there would have been no additional value created (and Saruman and Galadriel would never have been able to agree anyway). The point N is where the optimal investment is. It is the tangency point between the interest rate line and the production function. In other words, at the point N, the slope of both is the same. Investing in the production function gives the same return as investing along the interest rate line.

Can we model this optimal point N? Again going back to high school geometry:

$$Slope = \frac{Perpendicular}{Base}$$

Hence,

$$1 + r = \frac{NN_0}{N_0 J}$$

and

$$1 + r = \frac{NN_0}{N_0 A + AJ}$$

$$N_0 A + AJ = \frac{NN_0}{1 + r}$$

$$AJ = \frac{NN_0}{1 + r} - N_0 A$$

But NN_0 is the amount returned by the production function in the next season. $N_0 A$ is the initial value of the investment, and AJ is the additional value created by the interest rate line, which we will define as the Net Present Value (NPV) of the investment. Substituting, this gives our NPV formula:

$$NPV = \frac{CF_1}{1 + r} - I \qquad (2.1)$$

Where CF is a cash flow variable, $1/(1 + r)$ is a discount factor including a rate of interest, r, and I is the initial cost or outlay for the project/investment.

The NPV Formula

This single formula is the basis for almost everything we do in corporate finance. Translating our island terms into financial terms, the castaways are shareholders, potatoes are money, the initial potatoes are the initial dollar holdings, planting potatoes is like investing, eating potatoes is like receiving and spending dividends, and the potato exchange is a financial market.

This example has several takeaways. First and most important, capital markets allow managers to separate the consumption decision of shareholders from the investment decision of the firm. This principle, called the Fisherian separation theorem (after Irving Fisher who articulated this principle in 1930)[14] is one of the most important principles in finance. It states that the firm's investment decision is independent of the consumption preferences of the owner. The firm should make the investment decision that maximizes its present value, independent of owner preferences. The owners (shareholders) can then achieve their own optimal preferences by borrowing and lending on the capital markets as appropriate.

Second, this example shows how financial markets add value. They take deposits from long-term investors and lend them to short-term investors, earning the interest rate r, in the process. So, one of the most important roles of a financial intermediary, such as a commercial bank, is the transformation of money over time. If an investor needs short-term funding, the bank uses long-term deposits to convert long-term funds to short-term. If an investor has short-term deposits, the bank converts it into long-horizon returns. It also implies that banks should not earn economic rents[15] above the rate r, simply for the transformation role they perform.

To come back to our original question, which shareholders should the manager try to satisfy, the answer is that it does not matter. Managers need to just focus on maximizing NPV, given by equation 2.1.

This equation needs three inputs, two obvious and explicit and one not so obvious. The two obvious inputs are the cash flows, CF and the interest rate, r. The not-obvious (implicit) input is the financing decision of the firm – how the firm chooses to raise funds to invest in the investment opportunity. As we will see in the chapter on capital structure, we usually take the capital structure into account in the discount rate (the interest rate). The discount rate itself is determined by investors; we will see how this is derived in the next chapter, using portfolio theory and the capital asset pricing model.

What about the cash flows? It turns out that we have only four types of cash flows in corporate finance: single lump sums, annuities, perpetuities, and continuously compounded cash flows. Of these, the first three are most commonly used in corporate finance applications, while the last is typically used in option pricing. An example of a single lump sum is a single cash flow received a few years off. For example, if you expect an inheritance of £10,000 three years from now, that is a single lump sum. The present value will be

$$PV = \frac{FV}{(1+r)^T} = \frac{10,000}{(1+r)^3}$$

where FV is the future value, r is the discount rate, and T is the number of periods till we receive the future value. The future value is obtained by inverting the present value formula. In the example above, $10,000 = PV(1 + r)^3$.

In general, the PV is given by

$$PV = \frac{FV}{(1+r)^t} \qquad (2.2)$$

and the FV is given by:

$$FV = PV \times (1+r)^t \qquad (2.3)$$

An annuity is a series of cash flows that (1) are constant, (2) end after a while, and (3) earn the same interest rate throughout. In this case, the present value is given by:

$$PV = \frac{C}{r}\left(1 - \frac{1}{(1+r)^T}\right) \qquad (2.4)$$

where C is the periodic cash flow, r is the discount rate, and T is the number of periods the annuity lasts. So, for example, if you win a lottery that pays you ¥1,000 per year over the next 10 years, the present value is

$$PV = \frac{1,000}{r}\left(1 - \frac{1}{(1+r)^{10}}\right)$$

Since the present value is now a lump sum, the future value of an annuity is given by equation 2.3 above (multiply both sides by $(1 + r)^t$).

Finally, a perpetuity is a series of cash flows that stay the same, earn the same interest rate over time, and never end. So how can we find the value of an infinite stream of cash flows? Pretty easily as it turns out. What we want to do is find the value of

$$PV = \frac{CF_1}{(1+r)^1} + \frac{CF_2}{(1+r)^2} + \frac{CF_3}{(1+r)^3} + \cdots$$

Since the cash flows are the same, we can write

$$PV = \frac{C}{(1+r)^1} + \frac{C}{(1+r)^2} + \frac{C}{(1+r)^3} + \cdots$$

Multiplying both sides by $1 + r$, gives us

$$PV(1+r) = C + \frac{C}{(1+r)^1} + \frac{C}{(1+r)^2} + \frac{C}{(1+r)^3} + \cdots$$

which is the same as

$$PV(1+r) = C + PV$$

simplifying to

$$PV = \frac{C}{r} \qquad (2.5)$$

We can go back and derive the value of an annuity as the difference between two perpetuities, one starting next year and the second starting t years from now (when the annuity ends). The difference gives us a set of cash flows that begin next year and end after a set period of time.

Finally, slightly esoterically, we also have an alternative approach where we still have the same cash flows (single lump sums, annuities, or perpetuities) but we compound more than once a period. The reason this is esoteric is because we can always use equations 2.2 to 2.5 to compute the present and future values of these cash flows, as long as r is the discount rate over the period. For example, if the monthly interest rate is

1% (interest is paid every month), the value of investing $100 today with a repayment due one year from today is $100 \times (1 + 0.01)^{12} = \$112.68$, a straightforward application of equation 2.3. Unfortunately, sometimes banks and other intermediaries quote us annual rates but charge interest monthly.[16] You might be told for example, that the annual percentage rate (APR) is 12% compounded monthly. What that means of course is that the monthly rate is 1% but the former sounds grander and more complicated. Regardless, the equation for working directly with annual quoted rates is

$$FV = PV \times \left(1 + \frac{APR}{m}\right)^{m \times t} \qquad (2.6)$$

where m is the number of compounding periods per year.

This is pretty much equation 2.3 with r replaced by APR/m and t replaced by $m \times t$. Taking the example above, if the APR is 12 and the interest rate is monthly, the value of $100 to be received one year from today is $100 \times (1 + 0.12/12)^{12 \times 1} = 112.68$, the same as before. Why is this important? Well, it is only important when we shrink the compounding period further and further. For example, suppose we get interest paid every hour (as opposed to once a month). Since there are 8,760 hours in a year, the formula becomes $100 \times (1 + 0.12/8,760)^{8760 \times 1} = 112.74959$. One interesting thing about this calculation is that the amount we earn does not go up significantly (by only 7 cents here). Suppose we get interest paid every second. Surely, the amount goes up dramatically? Actually not. There are 31,536,000 seconds in a regular 365 day year, so the formula becomes $100 \times (1 + 0.12/31,536,000)^{31536000 \times 1} = 112.7496851$, about a 100th. of a cent more.

If paying interest over shorter and shorter time periods was purely a historical novelty, why do we care? It turns out that we can make the compounding period arbitrarily short (billionths of microseconds for example) but still end up with a finite value. If we compound in continuous time, the future value formula becomes

$$FV = PV\, e^{rt} \qquad (2.7)$$

where e is the exponential operator. Using this formula, the value of $100 to be received one year from today is 100 × $e^{0.12 \times 1}$ = $112.7496852. As you notice, there is not really very much difference between this and the compounding every second case, but it is the maximum that anyone can earn over any compounding period. And perhaps the difference is small for $100, but if we are talking about $100 million dollars, the difference is as large as 1.5 cents.[17] Economists like formula 2.7 because this is the limit on the interest we can earn regardless of how frequently we can compound. More to the point, it is also very easy to use.[18]

In particular, the term we will use as a shortcut is the flip side of equation 2.7:

$$PV = \frac{FV}{e^{rt}} = FVe^{-rt} \qquad (2.8)$$

So if you see something that looks like Xe^{-rt}, all it means is the present value of X today. It is the continuous time equivalent of equation 2.2

$$PV = \frac{FV}{(1+r)^t}$$

Having finally derived equations 2.7 and 2.8, we will now proceed to ignore them completely till we get to the Chapter 5 on option pricing theory, where we will use them extensively.

To summarize, in effect, we actually have only one equation (equation 2.1), from which we can derive all the other equations. And all corporate managers do is determine the cash flows, figure out what type of cash flow it is, and blindly apply equation 2.1 (after finding out the capital-structure adjusted discount rate). If the NPV is positive, the manager makes the investment, otherwise not.

What are examples of these types of cash flows? Consider the three most common types of cash flows that managers and investors try to value – the value of a share, the value of a bond, and the value of the company as a whole. The cash flows that investors receive once they buy a share are dividends. They also earn capital gains (or losses) if they sell the share for more (or less) than the amount paid for it. But why would some other investor buy the share, and what price would she pay? Well, the second investor buys the share to get dividends in turn plus capital gains when she sells it to a third investor, who in turn has the same motivation. Since no investor is the last investor for a share, the cash flows for a share consist entirely of dividends. The present value of a share is the present value of *all* future dividends paid by the firm forever. How do you compute the value of an infinite stream of dividends that are varying all the time? The answer is that you cannot. So we make simplifying assumptions, in particular, we assume that the dividends grow at a constant rate in the very long term. Then we can apply a growing perpetuity formula (a variant of equation 2.5) to value the current share price as

$$P = \frac{Div}{r - g}$$

where Div is next year's expected dividend payment, r is the discount rate, and g is the growth rate. This is called the Gordon Growth model, but it is really just a perpetuity formula in disguise.

A bond just consists of a series of annual coupon payments and a final face value repayment. So the price of a bond is the value of an annuity (the annual coupon payments are usually the same every year) and the value of a single lump sum (the face value). So the value of a bond is a combination of equations 2.4 and 2.2

$$P = \frac{C}{r}\left(1 - \frac{1}{(1+r)^T}\right) + \frac{FV}{(1+r)^T}$$

where C is the coupon amount, r is the discount rate (called the yield to maturity for a bond), FV is the face value, and T is the time to maturity.

Finally, what are the cash flows for a firm? We call this the free cash flow (FCF) and define it as the after-tax value of earnings before interest and taxes (EBIT) to which we add depreciation, subtract capital expenditure and subtract increases in working capital.

This sounds complicated, so let us simplify by considering the income statement of a small restaurant. The restaurant makes daily sales of £100 and incurs costs of £40 (on vegetables, meat, and other perishables). In addition, it depreciates its freezer and other equipment by £10 to account for wear and tear. Now its EBIT is defined as Sales − Costs − Depreciation, so in this case, it is equal to £100 − £40 − £10 = £50. The restaurant further pays interest expenses to its bank of £20 to get Earnings Before Taxes (EBT) and finally pays taxes at 50%. So the final bottom line figure is the firm's net income given by EBIT − Interest − Taxes = £50 − £20 − 50% × (£50 − £20) = £15.

What do the shareholders get? Well, first of all, they don't actually spend money on wear and tear − the manager will repair the freezer if it breaks, but that is actual expenditure incurred at the time when the restaurant repairs or replaces the freezer. So depreciation is not actually spent, and the shareholders in the restaurant can use it for other purposes. So is £15 + £10 = £25 the total amount available to the firm? Not quite. The interest payment is also ignored. In fact, we pretend the firm has no debt whatsoever. Interest payments do have an impact on the value of the firm, but precisely how they matter is the subject of Chapter 4, on capital structure. For now, all we note is that the firm adjusts the discount rate for the debt the firm has. What this means is that for the FCF of the firm, we pretend that the firm has no debt and hence pays taxes directly on EBIT. So the formula for FCF is

$$FCF = EBIT(1 - t_c) + \text{depreciation} - \text{capital expenditure} - \text{increase in working capital}$$

where t_c is the corporate tax rate and working capital is defined as the current assets less the current liabilities of the firm.

Once we compute the FCF in each period, we then apply one or more of equations 2.2 through 2.5 to compute their present values.

It is important to realize that each of the six ideas in finance is intimately tied to the other five. I have already briefly mentioned how portfolio theory and capital structure are tied to NPV, but so are asymmetric information and market efficiency.

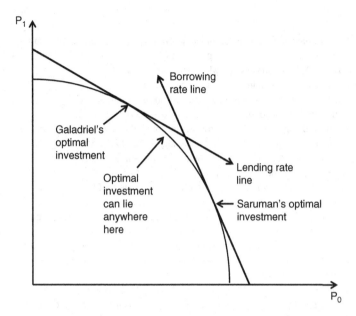

Figure 2.12 Borrowing and lending in the presence of asymmetric information

Let us suppose that there are a large number of informed investors on the market who know when an investment is likely to be good or not (for example, they may have more precise information on the shape of the production function). In setting interest rates, the market maker (banker) is worried that if the interest rate is too low, informed investors will borrow too much from him. Similarly, if the interest rate is too high, informed investors will lend too much to him. To protect himself, the market maker sets different borrowing and lending rates. The borrowing rate is higher than the lending rate. Sadly, as is shown in Figure 2.12, this destroys the idea of NPV.

The whole idea behind the Fisherian separation theorem was that managers could ignore investor preferences when deciding the optimal investment amount. Unfortunately, in the presence of asymmetric information (and different borrowing and lending rates), there is no unique investment amount that makes all investors better off. As we will see in later chapters, this has implications both for capital structure and for corporate governance.

Notes

1. Surveys have not been systematically conducted in less developed markets.
2. Perhaps because a significant proportion of American and British managers have MBAs from universities where their professors tell them that maximizing shareholder value is the only way to go.
3. Which is why you have been asked to organize the party.
4. Corporate jets, anyone?
5. Charles Duhigg and David Barboza, "In China, the Human Costs That Are Built into an IPad, *New York Times*, January 26, 2012, p. A1.
6. Jim Yardley, "Report on Deadly Factory Collapse in Bangladesh Finds Widespread Blame," *New York Times*, May 23, 2013, p. A5.
7. Simon Birch, "How Activism Forced Nike to Change Its Ethical Game," *Guardian*, July 7, 2012.
8. Max Nisen, "How Nike Solved Its Sweatshop Problem," *Business Insider*, May 9, 2013.
9. "The Stark Reality of iPod's Chinese Factories," *Daily Mail*, August 18, 2006, available at www.dailymail.co.uk/news/article-401234/The-stark-reality-iPods-Chinese-factories.html.
10. Another example of intertemporal consumption and investment decisions involving potatoes are those made by Matt Damon in the Hollywood movie *The Martian*. The production function in this movie is driven by what he can salvage/cannibalize from an abandoned space station to simulate a viable potato growing habitat. He does well until environmental factors literally blow his operation away. Completely consistent with our discussion in this chapter, Matt effectively calculates intertemporal consumption, using a preference curve tangency concept with the production function.
11. They get rescued in season three.
12. I'm indifferent between the two terms.
13. His senior business partner, Sauron, is known to be notoriously controlling and has terminated many a business partnership early – and permanently.
14. Irving Fisher, *The Theory of Interest: As Determined by Impatience to Spend Income and Opportunity to Invest It* (New York: MacMillan Co., 1930).
15. In economics, a rent is a payment in excess of the normal returns generated in competitive markets.
16. Why did banks even pay interest more than once a year? We will touch on this issue in Chapter 6 on asymmetric information, but essentially it was due to deposit insurance. Typically, banks keep only a small proportion of their assets as cash, lending out the rest. If there is a banking panic, each individual bank's customers rush to withdraw their money, forcing the bank into bankruptcy even when the bank is potentially healthy. Deposit insurance helps break the cycle because the government steps in to assure depositors that their deposits in the bank are guaranteed. Even if the bank goes bankrupt, the taxpayers will pay for the depositors to be made whole. Unfortunately, this means that the lenders have no incentive to monitor the bank because their deposits are protected. In addition, the bank now

has incentives to indulge in reckless lending behavior, in particular through competitive rate wars. In the United States, one of the provisions of the Glass-Steagall Act, Regulation Q, was to place limits on the interest rates banks could offer on deposits. Banks could still compete by changing the compounding period. As you can see, this is not extremely effective in raising the interest a depositor gets, but it may have been a good marketing tool. You can imagine bank advertisements: "I can offer you 5.25% interest." "Well, I can also offer you 5.25% but I'll pay you interest twice a year." "Oh, yeah? Well, we can offer you interest paid every day. And a free toaster." And so on. Anyway, U.S. interest rate ceilings were eventually phased out after the Depository Institutions Deregulation and Monetary Control Act in 1980.

17. Okay, perhaps that is not very large either but suppose the interest rate is not 12% but 24%? The difference goes up *twice* to 3 cents. Ah, but if the amount is actually a billion? Anyway, you get the idea.

18. Economists are smart *and* lazy.

3 | Portfolio Theory and the Discount Rate

Learning Points

- ■ What is the discount rate? An intuitive explanation
- ■ Measuring risk
- ■ Computing the expected return and variance for one security
- ■ Computing the expected return and variance for a portfolio of securities
- ■ Deriving the capital asset pricing model

What Is the Discount Rate? An Intuitive Explanation

In Chapter 2, we discussed the major inputs into the NPV formula (equation 2.1): The two obvious inputs are the cash flows and the discount rate (the non-obvious input – the capital structure of the firm – will be discussed in Chapter 4, on capital structure).

The cash flows are given by the characteristics of the asset. Suppose our investor, Galadriel (from Chapter 2, now rescued from the island) expects a cash flow of $100 as a dividend from a popular ring and assorted jewelry firm, Sauron Inc., two years from now. Unfortunately, it is not a certain $100 – there is a 50% probability that the firm will actually pay $200 and a 50% probability that the firm will pay nothing. The expected value of the payoff is 50% × 200 + 50% × 0 = 100.

Galadriel has to figure out how much she will value a cash flow like this. Obviously it will be risky, riskier than one from another (safe) firm, Elf River Associates (a retirement community), which promises a certain cash flow of $100 two years from now. But how much risk does Sauron really have? And how much tolerance for risk does Galadriel have?

Let us suppose that Galadriel is willing to pay $90 for the shares of Elf River. This means that she is getting $10 as interest over a period of two years. Applying equation 2.3, this tells us that

$$100 = 90 \times (1 + r)^2$$

which gives a value of r = 5.4%. This is the discount rate for this investment for Galadriel.

Now take Sauron Inc. The payoffs two years from now are risky. Rings are made of expensive material, and without adroit marketing, customers may never be persuaded to buy large numbers of rings. Therefore, there is some possibility that the firm will never pay dividends and some possibility that the firm will pay much larger dividends than before. Most investors when faced with this type of uncertainty would likely pay less than $90 for this stream of cash flows. Let's suppose Galadriel is willing to pay $85 for this stream. Then again applying equation 2.3, we have

$$100 = 85 \times (1 + r)^2$$

which gives a value of r = 8.5%.

In these two examples, what is interesting is that economists never observe the discount rate. They observe prices people are willing to pay and work the formula in reverse to derive the discount rate or required rate of return using equation 2.3 (or the other formulae in Chapter 2 for other types of cash flows). It is intuitive that faced with a risky investment, people will be willing to pay a lower price for the same payoff. But as we saw above, that means they will need a higher discount rate to be persuaded to buy the asset.

This is sometimes interpreted as the well-known dictum in financial markets: High returns mean high risks. This implies that if you want to make high returns, you need to take higher risks. But it is important to realize that finance theory says nothing of the sort. Taking higher risks does not necessarily get us higher returns. All finance theory actually says is that if an asset's payoffs are high risk, people will pay less to buy the asset, which only implies that high risks go hand in hand with lower prices (or higher expected returns), *not* the other way around.

But this gives rise to another obvious problem. Different investors may measure risk in different ways, or have different expectations of the probabilities of payoffs, or be less or more risk-averse. For example, Saruman may be much more risk loving than Galadriel. He may also be more optimistic that Sauron will actually pay dividends two years from now. For example, Saruman may think there is a 70% probability that Sauron will pay dividends and only a 30% probability that Sauron will not. Or Saruman may find gambling fun and derive more pleasure from taking a risk than Galadriel does. If Saruman is willing to pay $88 for Sauron Inc., the value of Saruman's discount rate would be given by

$$100 = 88 \times (1 + r)^2$$

which is 6.6%. Note that we cannot actually find out how much of the $3 difference in prices between Galadriel and Saruman is due to Saruman's lower risk aversion and how much is due to the fact that they expect different probabilities of success. In the best-case scenario, all we know is the price they were willing to pay. And in reality, we know even less, as explained below.

So coming back to our problem, what is the right discount rate for Sauron Inc.? Is it 6.6% or 8.5%? There are two ways to finesse this problem. One way is to assume that investors are homogenous. They are a bunch of clones (not clowns), with identical expectations and levels of risk aversion. In other words, they estimate the probabilities of success and failure identically and react to risk in the same way. This seems vaguely unsatisfying because we *know* that investors are different.

The second way is thinking through what happens when Galadriel offers $85 for a share in Sauron while Saruman offers $88. If the seller is selling one share, who gets it? Well, it certainly won't be Galadriel. In fact, we won't even see Galadriel's offer (or any other offer below Saruman's price). If Saruman is the highest bidder, then the only price recorded will be the price Saruman paid. And the discount rate will be set by Saruman's trade, which will be 6.6%. In this case, Saruman is the marginal investor. In finance theory, we can then pretend that the marginal investor is a large diversified pension fund. This has two advantages: Pension funds typically do not have to deal with taxes, so we can avoid tax complications, and they have large diversified holdings of shares, so we can assume that they are effectively risk neutral.[1]

Making this assumption gets rid of the risk-aversion problem. A large pension fund will be willing to pay the most for Sauron's shares because it is sufficiently diversified that it does not mind the risk involved in buying Sauron's shares over Elf River's. Hence the price it pays sets the discount rate. This still leaves the probability estimation problem (different investors may believe that the probabilities of Sauron succeeding or failing are different). We get around that by assuming that investors process information identically. They start out with the same probabilities and update their beliefs identically when new information comes in. Again this is not entirely satisfying because as we will see later on, in Chapter 7, on market efficiency, investors are different in the way they process information. Even large pension funds are run by human managers[2], who have similar biases to those of non-institutional investors.

For now, however, we are going to keep these two assumptions in the back of our heads – investors have homogenous expectations, and the marginal investor is a large diversified pension fund – and turn our attention to the fundamental problem in this chapter. How do we measure risk?

Measuring Risk

One of the most intuitive ways to explain the concept of risk is to examine the distribution patterns of returns earned by various assets as a histogram. A histogram is a way of representing the number of times a particular outcome occurs.

For example, suppose we can see the historical record for Sauron Inc. In the last 10 years, Sauron has earned its investors the following returns: 3.4%, −0.1%, 6.3%, 9.2%, 9.3%, −0.9%, −0.6%, −9.4%, 0.7%, and 1.7%.

These are all annual returns. They are computed by assuming that we bought the share on January 1 of the year and sold it on December 31 that year. During the year, we also earned dividends from the stock. For example, buying Sauron at $120, earning dividends of $9.10 during the year, and selling at $115 gives us a loss of $5 from buying and selling the stock. However, combined with the dividend, it gives a total return of $115 + $9.10 − $120 = $4.10. Dividing by the initial amount gives us a percentage return of 4.1/120 = 3.4% which is the first number in the return series. In most cases, we are not going to be buying and selling the stock every year, so these are actually hypothetical returns that would have been realized by someone who did, in fact, buy and sell the shares over the year.

Next, plotting the frequency with which these returns occur gives us a histogram (see Figure 3.1). In the histogram, a set of bins or intervals is chosen (here each bin is 2 percentage points wide, e.g., two consecutive intervals would be (8,10], (10,12], and so on – the mismatch between the rounded and square brackets in the intervals is a mathematical convention that tells us which of the two numbers lies within the interval). Then we

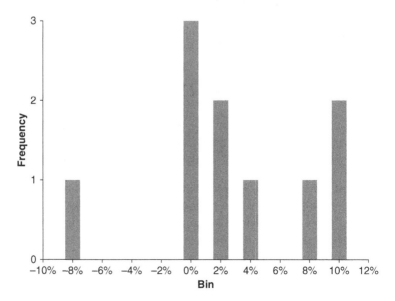

Figure 3.1 Histogram for annual returns on Sauron Inc.

simply count up how many past returns fall into each bin. For example, there are only two numbers that fall into the 8%–10% bin and so on. The histogram plots the distribution of returns.

In our example, we had ten annual returns. But we can go further. If we compute monthly returns, there are 120 numbers we can put into the histogram. If we go back to 1926 (the year from which we have detailed stock price records recorded by the Center for Research in Security Prices (CRSP) at the University of Chicago), we have over 1,000 return observations for the CRSP value weighted index (including dividend distributions) till December 2014. Suppose we plot all these monthly returns for the Dow Jones stock index over the eighty-nine-year window. What does the histogram look like? This histogram is illustrated in Figure 3.2.

At first glance, the histogram looks remarkably like a normal distribution. A normal distribution is called normal because a huge number of natural phenomena can be roughly represented by this distribution.[3] The most important characteristic of the normal distribution is that it can be completely described by

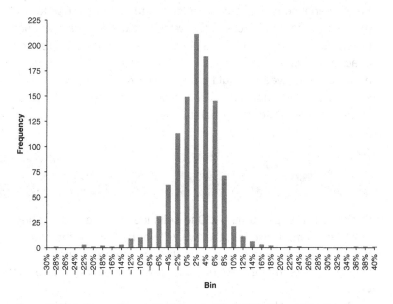

Figure 3.2 Histogram for monthly returns on the CRSP value-weighted index.
Data from CRSP

knowing only two of its parameters, its mean (the average value around which the histogram is centered) and its standard deviation (roughly measuring how wide the distribution is). If we know these two numbers, we can discuss with some confidence exactly how likely it is that a particular asset will earn a return within a certain range. For example, if the distribution of returns for large company stocks has a mean of 13% and a standard deviation of 20%, then we can say that there is a 68% probability that the returns next year will lie within one standard deviation of the mean, a 95% probability that the returns will lie within two standard deviations and a 99% probability that the returns will lie within three standard deviations. So you can tell your client with confidence that there is a less than a 1% chance that the return will be worse than −47% (13% − 3 × 20%) (i.e., there is almost no chance that the client will lose more than half her money). It makes you sound precise and authoritative.[4]

So making the assumption that asset returns are normally distributed, leads to the conclusion that only two parameters of a stock matter – its average (or expected return) and its standard deviation (or its squared term, called the variance). So the variance or standard deviation is taken as the risk to a particular stock. Investors in this world are called mean-variance investors, since they only care about these two parameters. And in addition, we assume that holding the level of risk constant, every rational investor would prefer higher returns to lower returns. Similarly, holding the return constant, every rational investor would prefer lower risk to higher risk.[5]

Computing Expected Return and Standard Deviation for One Security

Consider two separate firms. One sells ice-cream and the other sells raincoats. Obviously, the two will not be busy at the same time. Few people eat ice-cream in the rain, and fewer people wear raincoats in bright sunny weather when ice-cream is selling well.

A $100 investment in the ice-cream company returns an amount of $110 in sunny seasons but loses money, returning

$98, in rainy seasons. The raincoat company returns the same amount but in opposite weather. Finally, consider a $100 investment in government bonds. The bonds are riskless, in that the payoff of $103 is the same regardless of the weather.

Suppose there is a 50% chance of sunny weather[6] and a 50% chance of rainy weather. The expected payoff of the ice-cream company is 50% × $110 + 50% × $98 = $104 on an investment of $100. Hence, the expected return of the ice-cream company is (($104 − 100)/$100) = 4%. The variance measures how much the ice-cream company deviates from this expected value. After all, the ice-cream firm *never* makes a return of 4%. It makes 10% ((110 − 100)/100) in sunny weather and loses 2% ((98 − 100)/100) in rainy weather.

So what is the deviation from the expected return? In sunny weather, the ice-cream company returns 6% (10 − 4) *more* than the expected return, while in rainy weather, it returns 6% (4 − (−2)) *less* than the expected return. If we just take the average of these two numbers, we get zero ((6 − 6)/2 = 0) which would lead us to believe that the ice-cream always pays its expected return and that it is very safe. But that is not true. To get rid of the negative numbers, we square them.

So the variance is defined as the square of the deviations from the mean weighted by their probabilities. In this case, it would be

$$50\% \times (10\% - 4\%)^2 + 50\% \times (4\% - (-2\%))^2 = 0.0036 = 36\%^2$$

Unfortunately, 36 is in percent square terms, and it is difficult to compare the variance to the expected return of 4%. So for the sake of comparison, we define the standard deviation as the positive square root of the variance. In this case, $\sqrt{0.0036} = 6\%$. Exactly the same calculations apply for the raincoat company in reverse (since it earns $110 in rainy weather and returns $98 in sunny weather), so it has the same expected return and standard deviation as the ice-cream company.

The government bond always returns a payoff of $103, so its expected return is 3% ((103 − 100)/100 = 3%), and its standard deviation and variance are both zero. All these numbers are summarized in Table 3.1.

Table 3.1 Expected return and standard deviation of investment in ice-cream and raincoat companies

Expected return and standard deviation of investment in ice-cream and raincoat companies investment	Value in sunny weather (p = 50%)	Value in rainy weather (p = 50%)	Expected profit	Expected return	Standard deviation of return
Ice-cream company $100	$110	$98	50% × 110 + 50% × 98 = $104	$\frac{104-100}{100} = 4\%$	$\sqrt{50\% \times (10-4)^2 + 50\% \times (4--2)^2} = 6\%$
Raincoat company $100	$98	$110	50% × 98 + 50% × 110 = $104	$\frac{104-100}{100} = 4\%$	$\sqrt{50\% \times (4--2)^2 + 50\% \times (10-4)^2} = 6\%$
Government bonds $100	$103	$103	$103	$\frac{103-100}{100} = 3\%$	$\sqrt{50\% \times (3-3)^2 + 50\% \times (3-3)^2} = 0\%$

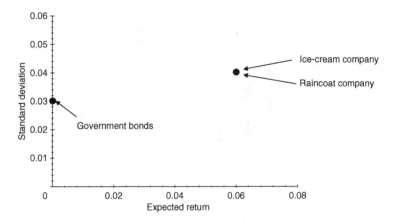

Figure 3.3 Expected return and standard deviation of the ice-cream and raincoat company

Which investment is preferable? Recall that both Saruman and Galadriel have different levels of risk aversion.[7] In Figure 3.3, we plot both the expected return and the standard deviation on a graph. Suppose Galadriel is extremely risk averse. Which investment would she prefer? She might just choose to invest in government bonds. Similarly, if Saruman is unbothered by risk, he might prefer an investment in either the ice-cream company or the raincoat company. Both will return a higher return than government bonds (4% as opposed to 3%) but will also involve taking higher risk. Which is better? The problem is that you can't tell because it depends on your level of risk aversion.

Now let us introduce a fourth possibility – to invest in a portfolio consisting of $50 in the ice-cream company and $50 in the raincoat company. As illustrated in Table 3.2, this portfolio returns $104 in either the rainy or sunny situation. This means that its standard deviation is zero – it never deviates from its expected return of 4%.

But instantly, we can see that this drastically narrows our preferred choice. In particular, Galadriel would prefer this investment over investing in government bonds, since this portfolio returns 4% with zero risk while the government bonds return 3% with zero risk. Similarly, Saruman also prefers the portfolio to individual investments in either the ice-cream or

Table 3.2 Expected return and standard deviation of investment in both ice-cream and raincoat companies

Investment	Value in sunny weather (p = 50%)	Value in rainy weather (p = 50%)	Expected payoff	Expected return	Standard deviation of return
Ice-cream company $100	$110	$98	50% × 110 + 50% × 98 = $104	$\frac{104-100}{100} = 4\%$	$\sqrt{50\% \times (10-4)^2 + 50\% \times (4--2)^2} = 6\%$
Raincoat company $100	$98	$110	50% × 98 + 50% × 110 = $104	$\frac{104-100}{100} = 4\%$	$\sqrt{50\% \times (4--2)^2 + 50\% \times (10-4)^2} = 6\%$
Government bonds $100	$103	$103	$103	$\frac{103-100}{100} = 3\%$	$\sqrt{50\% \times (3-3)^2 + 50\% \times (3-3)^2} = 0\%$
Investment in portfolio $50 in ice-cream company and $50 in raincoat company	$55 + $49 = $104	$49 + $55 = $104	$104	$\frac{104-100}{100} = 4\%$	$\sqrt{50\% \times (4-4)^2 + 50\% \times (4-4)^2} = 0\%$

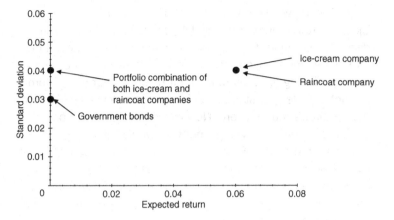

Figure 3.4 Expected return and standard deviation of the ice-cream and raincoat company

raincoat companies. Investing in the portfolio gives him the same return as investing in either of the individual investments (4%) but a much lower risk (0% as opposed to 6%). This situation is clearly illustrated in Figure 3.4.[8]

This is the essence of portfolio theory. All it says is that when investments are combined into portfolios, some level of risk disappears. This is because of diversification. In sunny weather, the raincoat and ice-cream companies earn negative and positive returns respectively, and these offset each other. No rational investor will hold some portfolio combinations – these combinations, called inefficient portfolios, are always dominated by other portfolio combinations. Assets are individually risky, but the risk goes down if you hold them within a portfolio.

Computing Expected Return and Standard Deviation for a Portfolio of Securities

What happens when we examine portfolios of securities? We will see that exactly the same conclusion holds. Some inefficient portfolio combinations will never be held. Hence, we can eliminate these portfolios from our analysis. But which portfolios are inefficient?

As before, we need to compute only two parameters – the expected return earned by the portfolio and its standard deviation. Consider two financial securities. One is a bond of Elf River Associates, and the other is a share in the well-known jewelry and ring firm, Sauron Inc. Elf River is safer than Sauron but not completely risk free. So its standard deviation is lower than Sauron's, but not zero. Now in a recession, not many people are likely to buy rings, but they would be willing to pay for a safe retirement. Similarly, in a boom, rings come into favor, raising Sauron's returns relative to Elf River.

Suppose the expected returns and standard deviations to the two firms in three states (a recession, normal times and a boom) are as in Table 3.3:

Computing as before, this gives us the expected return of Sauron as $20\% \times -7\% + 50\% \times 12\% + 30\% \times 28\% = 13\%$ and its standard deviation of $\sqrt{20\% \times (-7-13)^2 + 50\% \times (12-13)^2 + 30\% \times (28-13)^2} = 12\%$. Similarly, the expected return of Elf River is $20\% \times 12\% + 50\% \times 7.6\% + 30\% \times -4\% = 5\%$, and its standard deviation is $\sqrt{20\% \times (12-5)^2 + 50\% \times (7.6-5)^2 + 30\% \times (-4-5)^2} = 6\%$. Note that Elf River is safer than Sauron (lower standard deviation) but also has a lower return.

What is the expected return for a portfolio consisting of a 50% investment in Sauron and a 50% investment in Elf River? The general formula is

Expected return for a portfolio =
Fraction of total investment invested in asset 1 × the rate of return on asset 1 +
Fraction of total investment invested in asset 2 × the rate of return on asset 2 +

Table 3.3 Probabilities and returns earned in different states of the world

State of the world	Probability	Rate of return	
		Sauron	Elf River
Recession	20%	−7%	12%
Normal times	50%	12%	7.6%
Boom	30%	28%	−4%

Fraction of total investment invested in asset 3 × the rate of return on asset 3 + ⋯

Defining the fraction of the total investment in a particular asset i by the variable x_i, the expected return of a portfolio $E[R_p]$ is given by

$$E[R_p] = x_1 \times E[R_1] + x_2 \times E[R_2] + x_3 \times E[R_3] + \cdots \qquad (3.1)$$

where $E[R_1]$, $E[R_2]$, and so on are the expected returns to the individual assets. In this case, there are only two assets, so the expected return of the portfolio is 50% × 13% + 50% × 5% = 9%.

The formula for standard deviation of the portfolio is a little more complex. We first need to define a new term, the covariance. The covariance is a measure of how closely Sauron and Elf River move together. We need a measure that is large when Sauron and Elf River earn high returns together (or earn negative returns at the same time). In this case, the covariance should be large. This measure should also produce small positive or even negative numbers if Sauron and Elf River move in opposite directions. For example, if Sauron earns positive returns at the same time as Elf River earns negative returns, the covariance should be small or even negative.

The covariance is defined similarly to the variance. Recall that the variance measures the average squared deviation of an individual asset from its expected return. The covariance is defined as the product of the two individual deviations from the mean in the same state of the world.

In Sauron and Elf River's case, these calculations are illustrated in Table 3.4:

The covariance is given by 20% × (−20 × 7)%^{2} + 50% × (−1 × 2.6)%^{2} + 30% × (15 × −9)%^{2} = −0.007. Note that the negative covariance means that Sauron and Elf River are moving in opposite directions. If they were moving in the same direction, we would have either a bunch of positive numbers being multiplied by a bunch of positive numbers or a bunch of negative numbers being multiplied by another bunch of negative numbers (giving a positive number again). So the sum would typically be a large positive number if the two assets were moving together.

Table 3.4 Differences between overall expected returns and returns earned in different states of the world

		Deviation from expected rate of return	
State of the world	Probability	Sauron	Elf River
Expected return		13%	5%
Recession	20%	−7 − 13 = −20%	12 − 5 = 7%
Normal times	50%	12 − 13 = −1%	7.6 − 5 = 2.6%
Boom	30%	28 − 13 = 15%	−4 − 5 = −9%

It is important to note that the covariance is closely related to the variance. The variance of Sauron is its covariance with itself. Specifically, the variance of Sauron is 20% × (−20 × −20)%² + 50% × (−1 × −1)%² + 30% × (15 × 15)%² = 0.0148. Therefore, while we use the Greek letter σ_i to denote the standard deviation and σ_i^2 the variance of any asset i (since the standard deviation is the positive square root of the variance), the covariance is always defined for two separate assets. For two assets, i and j (Sauron and Elf River in this case), the covariance is denoted $\sigma_{i,j}$.

Putting it all together, the variance of the portfolio of two assets 1 and 2 is given by:

$$\sigma_p^2 = \left(x_1^2\sigma_1^2\right)+\left(x_2^2\sigma_2^2\right)+2\left(x_1\right)\left(x_2\right)\sigma_{12} \qquad (3.2)$$

To understand this intuitively, consider a large sack with a rabbit inside it. How much does the sack move? About as much as the rabbit. Now put an elephant into the sack with the rabbit. How much does the sack move now? Well, part of the movement is driven by the elephant and part by the rabbit. But the elephant is huge compared to the rabbit, so most of the perceived movement outside the sack will be driven by the movement of the elephant. Putting this into terms of equation (3.2), the proportions x_1 and x_2 of the portfolio are the total weights of the elephant and rabbit respectively, as a proportion of the total weight of both animals together, while the σ_i and σ_i tell us how much each animal moves by itself. Since x_1 is large, if the elephant is moving a lot, the movement of the elephant will have a large effect on the movement of the sack. In contrast, if the elephant does not move at all, it will have no effect on the movement of the sack, regardless of how large it is. The third item that affects the movement of the sack is how well the two animals react to each other. If they are hostile towards each other, there is likely to be much more movement than if they complement each other.[9] Having a negative covariance means that the two animals complement each other, hence they do not fight. Having a positive covariance means that they are similar, hence they fight a lot.[10]

Using the numbers for Sauron and Elf River, this works out as

$$\sigma_p^2 = (0.5^2 \times 0.12^2 + 0.5^2 \times 0.06^2 + 2(0.5) \times (0.5) \times 0.0148 = 0.0011$$

and the standard deviation is $\sqrt{0.0011} = 3.4\%$.

What is especially interesting is when we compare the three expected returns and the variances in Table 3.5.

The portfolio has a higher expected return than Elf River and a lower standard deviation – the best of all possible worlds. Elf River is therefore dominated by the portfolio. Are there other inefficient portfolios?

The answer is yes. To see this, all we need to do is vary the amounts of investment in our portfolio. Let us compute the expected return and standard deviation when we change the weight of the portfolio from 0% weight in Sauron (a portfolio consisting entirely of Elf River) to 100% weight in Sauron (no Elf River in the portfolio) in 10% increments. This is illustrated in Table 3.6.

Plotting these numbers on a graph gives us Figure 3.5. It is obvious from the graph that no rational person who prefers

Table 3.5 Comparing expected returns and standard deviation for the individual securities and the portfolio

Security	Expected return	Standard deviation
Sauron	13%	12%
Elf River	5%	6%
Portfolio	9%	3.4%

Table 3.6 Expected portfolio returns and standard deviation for different portfolio weights

Weights in Sauron	E[R$_p$]	σ$_p$
0%	5%	6%
10%	6%	4%
20%	7%	3%
30%	7%	2%
40%	8%	2%
50%	9%	3%
60%	10%	5%
70%	11%	7%
80%	11%	9%
90%	12%	10%
100%	13%	12%

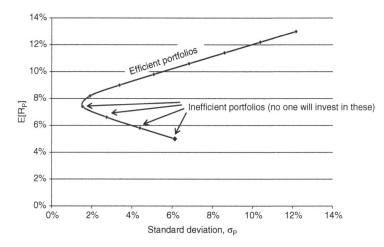

Figure 3.5 Portfolio risk and return combinations

higher returns to lower, and lower risk to higher will invest in any of the inefficient portfolios. They would only choose to invest in efficient portfolios.[11]

What happens when we have more than two assets in a portfolio? Well, computing the expected returns is straightforward. However, the variance is a little complicated because of the problem of computing the covariance. The covariance formula works only for two assets at a time since we can only tell if two assets are moving together or in opposite directions. If we introduce even one more asset, it is impossible to think, even intuitively, about how all three move together (Do two of the three move together, or do they all move independently?) So the only way to compute the variance is to compute the covariance for every possible pair of assets in the portfolio, weight them by the fraction of investment in each asset, and add up all the weighted covariances.

For three assets, we have nine possible pairs as in the matrix below, whereas before x_1, x_2, and x_3 represent the fraction of investment in the individual three assets and σ_{ij} represents the covariance between asset i and asset j. Also as before, σ_{ii} (or σ_i^2) represents the variance of i (the covariance between i and itself).

$$\left\{ \begin{matrix} x_1^2\sigma_{11} & x_2x_1\sigma_{21} & x_3x_1\sigma_{31} \\ x_1x_2\sigma_{12} & x_2^2\sigma_{22} & x_3x_2\sigma_{32} \\ x_1x_3\sigma_{13} & x_2x_3\sigma_{23} & x_3^2\sigma_{33} \end{matrix} \right\} = \left\{ \begin{matrix} x_1^2\sigma_1^2 & x_1x_2\sigma_{12} & x_1x_3\sigma_{13} \\ x_1x_2\sigma_{12} & x_2^2\sigma_2^2 & x_2x_3\sigma_{23} \\ x_1x_3\sigma_{13} & x_2x_3\sigma_{23} & x_3^2\sigma_3^2 \end{matrix} \right\}$$

since the off-diagonal covariance terms are equal to their corresponding terms on the other side. For example, $x_1x_2\sigma_{12} = x_2x_1\sigma_{21}$ and so on. Once we get all the terms, the variance of the portfolio is the sum of all these terms.

$$\sigma_p^2 = \left(x_1^2\sigma_1^2\right)+\left(x_2^2\sigma_2^2\right)+\left(x_3^2\sigma_3^2\right)+2\left(x_1\right)\left(x_2\right)\sigma_{12} + \\ 2\left(x_1\right)\left(x_3\right)\sigma_{13}+2\left(x_2\right)\left(x_3\right)\sigma_{23} \qquad (3.3)$$

Two conclusions are evident from this formula and from the matrix above The first conclusion is that the number of terms increases dramatically every time we add another asset. For 3 assets, we have $3 \times 3 = 9$ terms. For 10 assets, we would have $10 \times 10 = 100$ terms. For 100 securities, we would have 10,000 terms in our equation. However, the second conclusion is that each additional asset adds only one variance term (the item on the diagonal) but a large number of covariance terms (covariances with all the other assets individually). Again, for 100 assets, we have 100 variance terms and 9,900 covariance terms. If we add 1 more asset, we add 1 variance term but 200 covariance terms!

This is one of the most important things to bear in mind when we think of risk. In computing the risk of any portfolio, the individual variance terms are completely drowned by the covariance terms.

So now let us suppose we are plotting the return-risk combinations for all possible portfolios of all possible assets in the universe. What does the resulting graph look like? A lot like Figure 3.6. If we plot all possible combinations in the same expected-return/standard-deviation space, we can also draw the outermost convex hull of all these combinations as in Figure 3.6.

And again, rational investors will only care about the upper part of the convex hull – the set of efficient portfolios. So basically, of all the infinite number of possible portfolio combinations we can eliminate all the inefficient portfolios that lie on the lower part of the convex hull or within the convex space. Coming up with this elimination process earned Harry Markowitz a Nobel Prize in 1990.

Unfortunately, it was not enough. When we subtract the infinite number of inefficient portfolios from an infinite number of total portfolio combinations, we are left with an infinite number of efficient portfolios to choose from. Which is the best one? Again it depends on the investor's level of risk aversion, which is not entirely satisfactory.

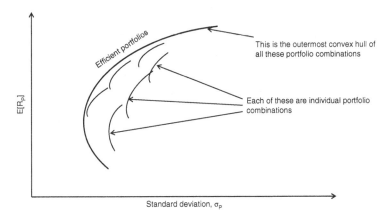

Figure 3.6 Portfolio risk and return combinations for all possible portfolios in the universe

There is one way out. When plotting all portfolio combinations of all the assets in the universe, we (inadvertently) left out one asset – the risk-free asset. What is a risk-free asset? According to economists, a risk-free asset is a government bond. But which one? There are millions of government bonds all over the world with varying maturities and denominated in different currencies. Similarly, lots of governments have defaulted on their debts. Surely these are not risk free?

It turns out that economists have a very precise idea on what a risk-free asset should do. First, you should always be able to get back your money – there should be no default risk. Is this true for all government bonds? Yes, if the bonds are issued in the local currency. For example, if you go to the U.S. government and demand payment of your maturing ten-year government bond, if the government has no money, it will simply call the mint, print out some money and give it to you. However, if the bonds are not issued in the local currency, this is not possible. For example, if Argentinean bonds are issued in U.S. dollars, the Argentinean government cannot print U.S. dollars when the bonds come due.

Second, inflation risk is not considered. If the government keeps printing money to meet the demands of creditors, the value of the money falls, resulting in inflation. But as long as we have our money (essentially a piece of paper back), our bond is risk-free.

Third, different maturities and currencies do not matter. Economists appeal to the no-free-lunch idea to justify this. For example, one variant of the no-free-lunch idea called uncovered interest parity, says that if domestic risk-free interest rates are different across two countries, exchange rates will adjust by the time the deposit comes due, thus leaving the investor indifferent between investing internationally or domestically. For example, a European investor might be able to invest in Europe at 2% and in the United States at 3%. If the European investor chooses to invest in the United States, she would need to convert Euros into U.S. dollars at the current spot exchange rate, invest in the United States, and reconvert into euros when the U.S. dollar deposit matures. If uncovered interest parity holds, the exchange rate at the maturity will have adjusted so that the investor will earn 2% on the U.S. deposit after both conversions. There are other variants involving forward contracts (covered interest parity), but the basic idea remains the same.

So now let us assume that we have an appropriate risk-free asset. What is the expected return and variance of a combination of a risk-free asset and any other portfolio? Well, the expected return is given by equation 3.1.

$$E[R_C] = x_F \times R_F + x_1 \times E[R_1] \tag{3.4}$$

where $E[R_C]$ is the expected return of the portfolio combination. Notice that we have got rid of the *expected* part of the return on the risk-free asset since it is risk free – we *know* what return we will get.

What about the variance of the combination, σ^2_C? The variance of the risk-free asset is zero (since the returns do not change depending on the state of the world). In addition, the covariance of any asset with the risk-free asset is also zero, since the returns of the risk-free asset do not change regardless of how the other asset is performing. Putting these two into equation 3.2 gives us

$$\sigma^2_C = \left(x_F^2 \sigma_F^2\right) + \left(x_1^2 \sigma_1^2\right) + 2\left(x_F\right)\left(x_1\right)\sigma_{F1} = 0 + \left(x_1^2 \sigma_1^2\right) + 0 = \left(x_1^2 \sigma_1^2\right) \tag{3.5}$$

Hence, the standard deviation of the combination is the square root of the variance or $x_1 \sigma_1$.

Putting both equations 3.4 and 3.5 together leads to a simple conclusion. Every combination of a risk-free asset and every other asset lies on a straight line in expected-return–standard-deviation space. But which one will investors pick? From Figure 3.7, the answer is obvious. No one will pick a combination of the risk-free asset and any portfolio that lies below the convex hull – the combination will be inefficient. For example, P_1 and P_2 are not viable portfolios. The only viable combination that offers the highest return for the minimum risk is the combination of the riskless asset with an efficient portfolio.

But which efficient portfolio? Since the efficient frontier is the convex hull of all the interior portfolios, it is easy to show that there will be only one point that derives from the tangent

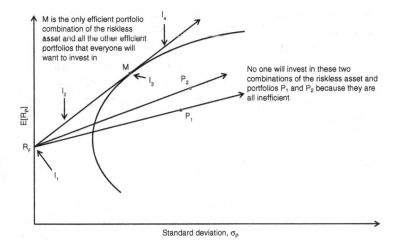

Figure 3.7 Portfolio risk and return combinations for any portfolio with the riskless asset

drawn from the risk-free asset to the efficient frontier. This is the portfolio M in Figure 3.7.

It is now easy to see that every investor will prefer investing in a combination of the risk-free asset and the portfolio M to any other efficient portfolio. For example, an investor who does not like risk at all, might invest 100% of his portfolio in the risk-free asset (I_1 in the figure). An investor who is moderately risk averse might invest 50% of her portfolio in the risk-free asset and 50% in portfolio M (I_2 in the figure). Someone who is relatively risk-tolerant might choose to invest all her money in the portfolio M (I_3 in the figure). And finally someone who is extremely risk-tolerant might choose to invest a negative amount (say −20%) in the risk-free asset[12] and invest more than 100% in the portfolio M (I_4 in the figure).[13]

In every single case, someone investing on the line connecting the risk-less asset R_F and M will be better off than someone investing in *any* other efficient portfolio. Therefore, all investors, regardless of their risk-preferences will choose a combination of R_F and M. The precise combination depends on their risk tolerances, but the two basic components of the optimal choice stay the same, the risk-free asset and portfolio

M. This fundamental insight earned William Sharpe the Nobel Prize in 1990 (along with Harry Markowitz mentioned earlier).

What is portfolio M? Well, it is just one particular tangential point on the efficient frontier, and the convention is to call it the market portfolio. If the rate of return on the risk-less asset changes, the market portfolio changes (since the tangent point changes).

Deriving the Capital Asset Pricing Model

Figure 3.7 can also be used to derive a version of the capital asset pricing model (CAPM). What is the expected rate of return on any portfolio on the line joining the risk-free asset and M? A cleaned up version of Figure 3.7 is in Figure 3.8.

From high-school geometry, the equation of a line is given by

$$y = intercept + slope \times x$$

Here, y is the variable measured on the y-axis, which is $E[R_p]$. The x axis measures the standard deviation for the portfolio, σ_p. The intercept is the point where the line touches the y-axis (the point when x = 0). In this case, it is R_F. Finally, the slope is given

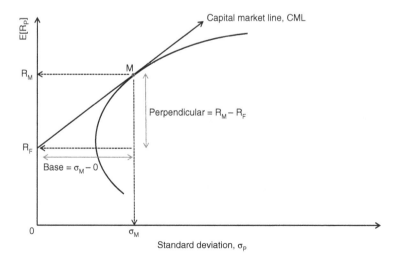

Figure 3.8 The capital market line

by the perpendicular/base of a right-angled triangle. And we have precisely such a right-angled triangle in Figure 3.8. So the slope is $(R_M - R_F)/(\sigma_M - 0)$.

Putting it all together, the expected return of any portfolio that investors will choose to invest in is given by:

$$E[R_P] = R_F + \frac{R_M - R_F}{\sigma_M} \times \sigma_P \qquad (3.6)$$

This is one version of the capital asset pricing model. But it is not the most well-known version, the version that we all know and love.[14]

To get that version, we need to backtrack a bit. Recall that in our discussion of equation 3.3, when we were trying to derive the standard deviation of a portfolio, we said that in computing the risk of any portfolio, the individual variance terms are completely drowned by the covariance terms. So what matters is the covariance, not the variance. But the covariance with what? Well, from the previous section, every investor in the world is holding a combination of the risk-free asset and the market portfolio, M. The covariance of any asset with the risk-free asset is zero. So the only thing that matters is the covariance with the market portfolio. This is the true measure of risk of an asset – how much it covaries with what the investor is already holding, the market portfolio.

What is the problem with just using the covariance of the asset with the market portfolio? Well, suppose the market is extremely volatile. The covariance will be large as well. But the asset's risk has not changed. So we need to get rid of the variance of the market. Specifically, we divide the covariance of the asset with the market portfolio by the variance of the market and call the ratio β.

$$\beta = \frac{\text{cov}(R_i, R_M)}{\sigma_M^2} = \frac{\sigma_{i,M}}{\sigma_M^2} \qquad (3.7)$$

We need one more step to get to the CAPM. Recall that the covariance of the risk-free asset with any other asset is zero. So the β of the risk-free asset is zero. Similarly, the covariance of any asset with itself is the variance. Substituting this in equation 3.7 leads to the conclusion that the β of the market portfolio is 1.

With all this background, we can now tackle the CAPM. Figure 3.9 is almost exactly the same as Figure 3.8 except that the x-axis is denoted in beta, β, terms, not in standard deviation, σ_p, terms.

Noting that the beta of the market portfolio is 1, the equation of the security market line (SML) is given by

$$E[R] = R_F + \frac{R_M - R_F}{1} \times \beta$$

Or in a more familiar form

$$E[R] = R_F + \beta \times (R_M - R_F) \tag{3.8}$$

This equation is the familiar CAPM. It tells us that if we know the risk-free rate, R_F, the market risk premium, $R_M - R_F$, and the beta of any asset, we can plug those numbers into the CAPM, and the discount rate will appear on the other side. This is the rate that is one of the two explicit inputs into the NPV formula.

One incidental side note we will need later: Because the SML is a straight line, *any* point on a straight line can be written as a linear combination of any two points on that line. What this

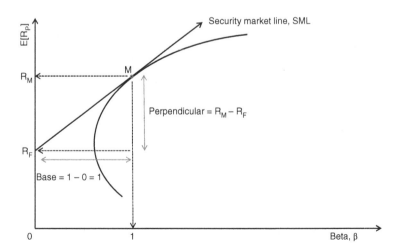

Figure 3.9 The security market line

means practically is that the beta of any portfolio is also a linear combination of the betas of its components.

$$\beta_P = w_1\beta_1 + w_2\beta_2 + w_3\beta_3 + \cdots \qquad (3.9)$$

where the w variables are the weights of the assets 1, 2, 3 ... in the portfolio.

What is the market portfolio, though? Unfortunately, we don't know. The market portfolio cannot be measured. It is a particular combination of all the assets in the universe. The problem is that some of those assets cannot be traded freely. For example, human capital (your education and skills) cannot be freely bought and sold in fungible quantities.[15] Similarly, houses are illiquid and sale prices hard to determine. So we take a very broad-based index such as the Russell 3000 index, the S&P500 index, or the CRSP value-weighted index, and assume[16] that these are close approximations to the true market portfolio.

Suppose the S&P500 is a good approximation of the market portfolio. Are our problems over? Not really. The number we need for the NPV formula in Chapter 2 is the expected discount rate (the left-hand side of equation 3.8 above). To compute this properly, we need two more terms in addition to the beta – the market risk premium, $R_M - R_F$, and the risk-free rate.

Unfortunately, we don't know the market risk premium either. So we make a second assumption – that over extremely long periods, the historical differences between returns on our market portfolio and the returns to the risk-free asset are stable enough to serve as good approximations to the future. But what does an extremely long time mean? You guessed it. We have no idea. Different academics have obtained prices going back over periods ranging from 80 to 100 years and have come up with different measures ranging from 5% to 8%. Basically, your choice as a corporate manager is to pick a number somewhere in that range and stick with it.

What about the beta? For future expected returns, we need the beta over the period of our investment in the future. But, of course, we don't know that either. So we make yet another assumption – that the firm's historical covariance over time with the market is constant and serves as a good proxy for expected beta. So we take a period (say the last five years), measure the covariance of the firm's historical returns with the market's returns over that period, and divide by the historical variance of the market in the same period. That gives us the historical beta, and we use it as a proxy for future beta.

Why five years? The trade-off we have is simple. Choosing a longer time period gives us more stable numbers for the beta. However, if the business environment is fast changing, using too long a period can lead to beta estimates that are completely irrelevant to the actual beta estimates we need. So a rough rule of thumb is that if the business is fast moving, pick a shorter period to compute beta (but not too short, otherwise the beta itself will be a noisy measure). If the business is stable and mature, a longer period is probably better.

The final punch line of this chapter is simple, however. The most important theoretical assumption we made to derive the CAPM is that investors are most concerned with mean returns and variances. If that assumption is correct, then the CAPM will tell us what the expected return is to any asset. That expected return is the discount rate we need in the NPV formula in Chapter 2.

But the story does not end here. The risk (now solely referring to beta) of the firm is also affected by leverage. To see why, we need the third major idea of corporate finance – capital structure theory.

Notes

1. A risk neutral investor is one who is indifferent between a certain payoff of $100 and a 50–50 gamble of $200 and $0.
2. At the time of writing.
3. If you want to get fancy, this is also called a Gaussian distribution, named after the German mathematician, Johann Carl Friedrich Gauss.
4. In reality, the distribution of returns is fat tailed – both extreme good and bad events happen a little more frequently than predicted by the normal distribution. Unfortunately, this empirical distribution is not mathematically very tractable, so we ignore it. This is not a major concern in most situations, since most of us are not so extremely highly levered that we will be significantly affected by a major market meltdown. For more reading on topics such as normal distributions, confidence levels, and hypotheses testing, any elementary statistics textbook will do.

5. Please feel free to contact the author if you prefer lower returns to higher returns. The author may have some interesting investment opportunities available.

6. This chapter was not written when the author was in England.

7. The level of risk aversion has nothing to do with their preferences for short- or long-term assets in the previous chapter.

8. Of course, such a situation would never persist in equilibrium. If two assets were both riskless and earned very different returns (the government bonds earning 3% and the portfolio earning 4%), you could make an unlimited amount of money (a free lunch) by borrowing at the government bond rate and buying the portfolio. Unfortunately, the basic underlying principle of finance is that free lunches do not exist. In real life, such a discrepancy would quickly disappear. Borrowing at the government bond rate would drive the price of the bond down (raising its return) and buying the portfolio would raise its price (driving its return down) till the two earned the same returns.

9. Like yin and yang. As an economist, I am not sure what precisely this is, but talking about it looks cool.

10. At this point, this example is getting a little stretched, so we won't go into precise definitions of complements and opposites.

11. By the way, it is entirely possible for the weights to be negative. A negative weight implies that the investor is selling the asset short (borrowing it from someone else and selling it) and then using that money to invest a larger amount in the other asset. For example, if you had $100 to invest but wanted to buy $120 worth of Elf River, you would sell $20 of Sauron short ($x_1 = -20\%$) and invest the extra in Elf River ($x_2 = 120\%$). All that matters is that the weights should sum to 100%. Economists like to think that, much like matter and energy, money cannot be created or destroyed, a concept that makes us as smart as physicists.

12. 120% to be precise, since the percentages have to add up to 100%.

13. How can someone invest a negative percentage in the risk-free asset? Simple. Suppose the investor starts out with $100. The investor borrows $20 at the risk-free interest rate and invests $120 in the portfolio M.

14. Not really.

15. For example, you cannot sell three units of your MBA and four units of your undergraduate degree to anyone else.

16. Pretend.

4 Capital Structure Theory

Learning Points

- Why does leverage affect the discount rate? An intuitive explanation
- Capital structure in perfect and efficient capital markets
- The Modigliani-Miller propositions
- Capital structure in the presence of taxes
- Trade-off hypothesis
- Pecking order hypothesis

Why Does Leverage Affect the Discount Rate? An Intuitive Explanation

So far, we have covered two of the six ideas underlying all of corporate finance: net present value (NPV) and the capital asset pricing model (CAPM). The NPV formula has two explicit inputs: the cash flows and the discount rate. The discount rate is given by the CAPM. So far, so good. However, this is not enough. The discount rate is also affected by a third, implicit, input – the amount of debt the firm has. The obvious explanation for this is that investors factor- in the risk that the firm will go bankrupt into their calculations and accordingly pay a lower price (demand higher returns) for a firm with a higher default possibility. Although this is quite true, it is not the entire answer. Investors will pay a lower price even for firms that have no bankruptcy risk if the firm has debt. This is because in many, if not most, business regimes, debt has to be paid off before ordinary equity holders can get their payoff. As an equity investor, leverage allows you to ratchet up your returns and reduce the money you yourself have at risk.

Consider an investment that returns a payoff of either $101 or $99 on an initial investment of $100. This would be a return of ±1%. Now suppose you borrow $99 from your mother and only invest $1 of your own money. Your mother, who is a very nice person, does not require any interest, but you would like to return her investment before you take your payoff. In other words, your mother's investment is like debt.

If the investment does well, you make $101, return $99 to your mother, and keep $2 for yourself. On your initial investment of $1, this represents a 100% return. Similarly, if the investment does badly, you make $99, return it all to your mother and keep nothing for yourself. You have basically lost all your money, a return of −100%. Overall, leverage has enabled you to transform a return of ±1% to a return of ±100%. You have the potential to make a lot of money but also to lose a lot of money. That is the primary source of increased risk to the equity holder in the presence of debt. This also represents a huge source of returns to many hedge funds and private equity firms. The next time you hear that a particular hedge fund is generating outsize returns, you may want to ask yourself whether these returns are being generated by superior ability or by leverage.

But precisely how much additional return is being generated by this additional risk? To answer that question, we need to turn to the third big idea in corporate finance – capital structure theory. Franco Modigliani and Merton Miller each won the Nobel Prize in Economics, in 1985 and 1990, respectively for coming up with this idea. Like all the ideas so far, the intuition is deceptively simple.

Capital Structure in Perfect and Efficient Capital Markets

To understand why the idea was awarded a Nobel Prize, let's start by thinking through what they were trying to establish. The basic question was to ask what is the ideal amount to borrow? More generally, firms have several options to raise the necessary cash to make an investment – they can issue equity, they can issue debt, or they can use retained earnings. What is the best approach?

At the time, empirical studies, analyzing both the time-series and the cross-section of firms, offered little or no guidance to this question. There appeared to be a large amount of time variation in the amount of debt raised by firms relative to equity. Similarly, there was a large amount of variation from one country to another. With no obvious patterns in the debt-equity ratio either across time or across countries, economists tested empirically whether firms issuing debt earned positive or negative returns at the time of issue. Unfortunately, there was no consistent pattern here either. Some firms issued debt and earned positive returns, leading to the implication that debt was a good idea. However, other firms issued debt and earned negative returns, leading to exactly the opposite conclusion.

What was going on? The problem is that firms don't just issue debt and then stop. They do something with the cash – they invest it in some kind of asset. If the asset has a negative NPV, however, the initial announcement of the debt issue will be greeted with a negative return – but the market will be reacting to the investment, *not* to the issue of debt. Modigliani and Miller's fundamental insight was to decouple the firm's investment decision from its financing decision.[1]

Modigliani and Miller started by making some simplifying assumptions. They assumed that markets are efficient, everyone has symmetric information, buyers and sellers cannot influence the price by trading the asset (the market is perfectly competitive), there are no transaction costs, no taxes (either personal or corporate), and no lawyers (no bankruptcy costs). After making all these assumptions (in admittedly an ideal world), they embarked on a thought experiment. Specifically, they considered only firms where the firm issued debt but then used that money to buy back shares. Or the firm issued equity and then used that money to retire its debt. In either of these two cases, the assets side of the balance sheet is untouched. So if the firm's value changed, it could only be from the direct effects of issuing or retiring debt.

In the actual thought experiment, they defined a number of terms. These were as follows:

1. The value of an all-equity financed firm is V_U (which was equal to E_U, the value of its equity). U stands for unlevered: that is, a firm with no debt.

2. A firm with identical assets[2] but partially financed with debt, D_L and equity E_L has the value V_L (where L stands for Levered). The weight of debt in the total amount of firm liabilities is therefore given by D_L/V_L (or D/V for short), and the weight of equity is $E/V = 1 - D/V$.
3. The corporate borrowing rate is r_D.
4. The expected return on equity (the cost of equity) is r_E.
5. In the special case of an all-equity financed firm (with value V_U), the cost of equity is r_0 (where the zero stands for zero debt).
6. The firm's overall cost of capital is the weighted average cost of capital (WACC).
7. The firm is in a steady state. In other words, without loss of generality, the amount of depreciation exactly equals the capital expenditure and the change in working capital. So the capital expenditure is sufficient to replace assets worn down by physical wear and tear over time (as accounted for by depreciation). Although this assumption is not strictly necessary, it simplifies the formula for the cash flow generated by the firm from all its activities. Specifically, the cash flow generated by the firm (called its free cash flow, FCF) is its earnings before interest and taxes (EBIT).

The WACC is then defined by

$$WACC = r_D \frac{D}{V} + r_E \frac{E}{V} \qquad (4.1)$$

Modigliani and Miller decided to answer three questions in this setup.

1. How did the value of the firm change when it levered up? In other words, was V_L different from V_U? Since the assets were identical, the only way the two would be different were if debt had some intrinsic value.
2. How did the expected rate of return on equity, r_E, change when the debt-equity ratio changed? Recall that in the absence of any debt, the expected rate of return on equity is r_0. Did this change, when the firm levered up?
3. What happened to the firm's overall cost of capital, its WACC, as the firm levered up?

Their answers to these three questions were extremely surprising. Their first proposition said that in a perfect and efficient capital market (no taxes and no lawyers), debt is irrelevant. In other words:

$$V_L = V_U \qquad (4.2)$$

However, their second proposition went on to say that shareholders do bear more risk when debt has to be paid off before the shareholders get paid (as in the intuition in the first section of this chapter). Hence, the rate of return demanded by shareholders goes up in the presence of debt, $r_E > r_0$. Their final proposition says that although the shareholders demand higher expected returns, this is offset by the lower returns demanded by bondholders, so the firm's overall cost of capital is exactly the same as before. In other words, WACC = r_0.

The essence behind the Modigliani-Miller proof is that no free lunch exists (no arbitrage). If two assets have the same payoff, they must have the same initial cost.

To derive their proof intuitively, think of the firm as a giant pizza worth $10. Initially, you own the whole pizza and can consume it, getting $10 worth of satisfaction from it.[3] Suppose you were to sell a portion, say half the pizza, to someone else. Call this person a bondholder. The efficient price you could charge would be $5. You could try to charge more, but the bondholder would not pay. You could charge less, but why would you if the bondholder is willing to pay? So now you are left with $5 in cash and $5 worth of pizza satisfaction. Overall, your position is unchanged. You could if you chose, buy more pizza worth $5 to restore your position to its original state. The key is that the value of the pizza does not change.

A straightforward objection would be that the two scenarios (pizza and firm) are not analogous. Specifically, issuing debt commits you to paying interest for the lifetime of the debt (you are on the hook for a series of annual interest payments). Selling the pizza does not commit you to any further pizza payments next year. Again the key is the efficient markets assumption. The bondholders pay you the present value of all interest payments they will receive (using equation 2.2 or 2.4). That is the value of the bonds you have issued. Essentially, in an efficient market, all securities are issued at zero NPV. Neither the seller nor the buyer is stupid in buying (or issuing) a security with a negative NPV. You can keep that money paid in by bond-holders and use that, not to invest in a real investment, but to pay off the bondholders. So, in fact, there is no future commit-ment with the bonds. In real life, of course, you would take the money and invest it in an opportunity with a positive NPV and keep the extra for yourself as a shareholder.

To see this more formally, consider investing in both the levered and unlevered firm. Specifically, let us buy 10% of the equity of the unlevered firm and 10% of the levered firm. Since the levered firm has both debt and equity, this means we buy 10% of the debt (bonds) and 10% of the equity of that firm. Since the market values of the two firms are V_U and V_L respec-tively, the costs of these two strategies are $0.1 \times V_U$ and $0.1 \times V_L \ (= 0.1 \times E_L + 0.1 \times D_L)$ respectively.

Now recall that both the firms' assets are identical. That means they both generate the exact same free cash flow, EBIT. So in return for the investment in 10% of the equity of the unlevered firm, you get 10% of this free cash flow = $0.1 \times$ EBIT.

What about the levered firm? Well, it depends on how much debt the levered firm has. Suppose the firm has issued its debt D_L at an interest rate r_D. Then the amount of interest is $r_D \times D_L$. As a bondholder, you own 10% of this stream. That means you get $0.1 \times r_D \times D_L$ as interest. The remaining amount (EBIT $- r_D \times D_L$) goes to the shareholders. But you own 10% of that stream as well. So you get $0.1 \times$ (EBIT $- r_D \times D_L$) as dividends. Adding the two together, your total payoff is $0.1 \times r_D \times D_L + 0.1 \times$ (EBIT $- r_D \times D_L$) = $0.1 \times$ EBIT, exactly the same as before. By the no-arbitrage principle therefore, the two strategies must have the same initial cost. In other words, $0.1 \times V_U = 0.1 \times V_L$ or $V_U = V_L$, which is proposition 1. What is especially interesting is that the interest rate or the amount of debt issued is completely irrelevant to the proof.

Let's put some numbers on this to make it easier. Suppose the firms both generate $100 of EBIT every year (they are very small firms). Owning 10% of the equity of the unlevered firm costs $0.1 \times V_U$ and returns $10 as dividends. There are no taxes, personal or corporate, so this entire amount flows straight through to the shareholder. Owning 10% of the equity and 10% of the debt of the levered firm costs $0.1 \times E_L + 0.1 \times D_L = 0.1 \times V_L$. Suppose the firm has issued $100 of perpetual debt at a 5% interest rate. So the firm generates $100 of EBIT and pays out $5 in the form of interest and $95 in the form of dividends. Since you own 10% of both streams, you get $0.50 of interest and $9.50 of dividends = $10 exactly the same as before.

Suppose the firm has actually issued $1,000 of perpetual debt at 8%. Then the firm uses its EBIT to pay $80 in the form of interest and $20 in the form of dividends. You get $8 and $2 in the form of interest and dividends respectively, again exactly the same as before. The amount of interest and debt do not matter. "What about the risk of bankruptcy if the firm issues too much debt?" I hear you ask.

Well, we assumed that we live in a perfect world where there are no bankruptcy costs and no taxes. This matters. There is a difference between bankruptcy risk and bankruptcy costs. Suppose there are no bankruptcy costs. The firm passes over seamlessly from the shareholders to the bondholders if the firm cannot pay its bondholders on time without the lawyers getting involved. Then the bondholders who are now the new shareholders will continue to carry out the same positive NPV projects as before (why should they give up money-making opportunities?). So the firm's value remains unchanged. Only the owners change. The costs of bankruptcy arise because the transition is not seamless. Each of the two sets of parties is trying to maximize its own payoffs, and so each party takes actions that destroy firm value (for example, investing in negative NPV projects and hiring lawyers to maximize their share of the pie). Darn lawyers.[4]

So in a perfect world, regardless of the amount of debt the firm issues and regardless of the amount of interest paid on the debt, the value of the firm remains unchanged.

We can look at this example another way as well. Suppose there is only one firm (an unlevered firm) earning an EBIT of $100 every year. As a shareholder, as usual, you own 10% of the equity, costing you $0.1 \times V_U$. The CEO announces the firm will issue $150 of perpetual debt at an interest rate of 20%. This means that from next year on, the firm will not be able to pay out its entire $100 of EBIT as dividends. Because it will have to pay its bondholders first, the total amount of dividends paid out will be $100 - 0.2 \times 150 = 70$. Since you own 10%, your dividend payment drops to $7. Should you be aghast?

Not really. The reason is that the firm has to do something with the money it raises. According to the Modigliani-Miller thought experiment, it is not allowed to invest the money in an asset. So it pays out the money directly to the shareholders in an equity-for-debt exchange. As a 10% owner, you get $15. What do you do with it? Well, you can invest it at an interest rate of 20%. That gives you an interest payment of $3, and you are just as well off as before. In other words, if the firm takes on leverage, you can undo it by lending. Where can you find an investment that pays 20%? Well, the firm has just issued $150 worth of bonds that are paying 20%. With your $15, you can buy 10% of those bonds.

Let's look at one final variant of this example. Suppose there is only one firm (a levered firm) earning an EBIT of $100 every year. The firm also has $150 of perpetual debt that it issued at an interest rate of 20%. You own 10% of the equity (none of the debt), costing you $0.1 \times E_L$. Because it is paying its bondholders first, the total amount of dividends paid out is $100 - 0.2 \times 150 = 70$. Since you own 10%, your dividend payment is $7. The CEO announces the firm will retire its debt next year allowing the firm to pay out its entire $100 of EBIT as dividends. So the dividends you get from next year will go up to $10. Should you rejoice?

Again, not really. Here the reason is that the firm has to get the money to retire the debt from somewhere, since according to the Modigliani-Miller thought experiment, it is not allowed to get the money by selling assets. So it approaches the shareholders for the money in a debt-for-equity exchange. As a 10% owner, you need to pay up $15.[5] Where do you get that money? You need to borrow it from somewhere.[6] What interest rate can you borrow it at? Because of the Modigliani-Miller assumptions (perfect world, symmetric information), you will need to pay precisely 20%. That means that of your annual dividend payment of $10, you have to pay up $3, giving you a final payoff of $7, and making you just as well off as before. In other words, if the firm gets rid of leverage, you can again undo whatever the firm does by borrowing, creating your own home-made leverage.

Modigliani-Miller's second proposition says that risk to equity goes up in the presence of leverage. In the first section to this chapter, we saw that this had nothing to do with bankruptcy risk. The risk to equity holders goes up even in the absence of bankruptcy, essentially because the equity base of shareholders is a smaller proportion of the total asset base of the firm, magnifying the returns the firm earns (either positively or negatively). The precise formula giving the return to equity is

$$r_E = r_0 + \left(r_0 - r_D\right)\frac{D}{E} \tag{4.3}$$

Since r_0 is larger than r_D (equity is riskier than debt because equity holders are paid at the end), $r_0 - r_D$ is positive, and D/E is positive as well. Hence, $r_E > r_0$. Rather than prove this formally, it is easier to illustrate it through an example. Consider the three different scenarios in Table 4.1.

In each scenario, the firm's assets are identical, so it earns exactly the same amount of EBIT. The only difference between three scenarios is the amount of debt (and the amount of equity = Total assets − Total debt) in the firm. Working through the table, the cost of equity increases from 20% in the unlevered case to 56% in the high-leverage case (scenario C). Note that

Table 4.1 Expected return on equity for different levels of leverage

	A	B	C
Expected EBIT	$200	$200	$200
Assets	$1000	$1000	$1000
Expected rate of return for equity of unlevered firm, r_0 = EBIT/Equity = EBIT/Assets	20%	20%	20%
r_D (assumption)	8%	8%	8%
Debt	$0	$500	$750
Equity	$1000	$500	$250
Debt-equity ratio	0	1	3
Interest paid on debt (at r_D)	$0	$40	$60
Net Income = EBIT − Interest	$200	$160	$140
Rate of return for equity of levered firm, r_E = Net Income/Equity	20%	32%	56%

rather than working through this with an example, we can prove it directly from equation 4.3. For example:

$$\text{Scenario B}: r_E = 20\% + (20\% - 8\%)\frac{1}{1} = 32\%$$

$$\text{Scenario C}: r_E = 20\% + (20\% - 8\%)\frac{3}{1} = 56\%$$

Why does the required return to equity holders go up? Because they are taking more risk. Consider what happens if the firm makes an actual EBIT, not of $200 but only $100. This is illustrated in Table 4.2 for the three different levels of leverage from Table 4.1.

As the table shows, the higher the level of debt, the larger the deviation from the expected rate of return. It is important to note that this works in both directions. If the firm makes an unexpectedly high EBIT (say $400, instead of $200), the higher the debt level, the higher the actual returns earned by the shareholders. That is easily seen from Table 4.3.

Table 4.2 Differences between expected and realized returns of equity when the firm earns lower returns than expected

	A	B	C
Actual EBIT	$100	$100	$100
Assets	$1000	$1000	$1000
Realized rate of return for equity of unlevered firm, $\tilde{r}_0$ = EBIT/Equity = EBIT/Assets	10%	10%	10%
r_D (does not change)	8%	8%	8%
Debt	$0	$500	$750
Equity	$1000	$500	$250
Debt-equity ratio	0	1	3
Interest paid on debt (at r_D) (no bankruptcy costs, so has to be paid)	$0	$40	$60
Net Income = EBIT − Interest	$100	$60	$40
Realized rate of return for equity of levered firm, $\tilde{r}_E$ = Net Income/Equity	10%	12%	16%
Expected rate of return, r_E	20%	32%	56%
Deviation from expected rate	−10%	−20%	−40%

Table 4.3 Differences between expected and realized returns of equity when the firm earns higher returns than expected

	A	B	C
Actual EBIT	$400	$400	$400
Assets	$1000	$1000	$1000
Realized rate of return for equity of unlevered firm, $\check{r}_0$ = EBIT/Equity = EBIT/Assets	40%	40%	40%
r_D (does not change)	8%	8%	8%
Debt	$0	$500	$750
Equity	$1000	$500	$250
Debt-equity ratio	0	1	3
Interest paid on debt (at r_D) (no bankruptcy costs, so has to be paid)	$0	$40	$60
Net Income = EBIT – Interest	$400	$360	$340
Realized rate of return for equity of levered firm, $\check{r}_E$ = Net Income/Equity	40%	72%	136%
Expected rate of return, r_E	20%	32%	56%
Deviation from expected rate	20%	40%	80%

To put this simply, leverage magnifies returns, good and bad. That is what increases risk to the shareholders. We can also relate this increase in risk to the CAPM directly. Recall that the risk in the CAPM is given by its beta. If the beta of the unlevered firm is given by β_U and the beta of the levered firm is given by β_L, then

$$\beta_L = \beta_U \left(1 + \frac{D}{E} \right) \qquad (4.4)$$

Where does this equation come from? Well, it actually comes from portfolio theory, specifically from equation 3.9. Recall that the beta of a portfolio is the beta of its components. Here the firm is a portfolio of its liabilities (I can buy the whole firm by buying all its debt and its equity). Therefore, the beta of the assets side of the firm must equal the weighted sum of the betas of the debt and the equity. But in an unlevered firm, there is no debt, so the beta of the assets must be equal to the beta of its equity. Putting this together,

$$\beta_A = \beta_U = \frac{D}{V} \beta_D + \frac{E}{V} \beta_E$$

Assuming the debt is risk-free (since there are no bankruptcy costs), we have $\beta_D = 0$. Since $\beta_E = \beta_L$, we therefore have

$$\beta_U = \frac{E}{D+E}\beta_L$$

or

$$\beta_L = \frac{D+E}{E}\beta_U$$

which is equation 4.4.

Plugging in the levered beta into the CAPM will give us the return to equity directly while plugging in the unlevered beta will give us the return to equity for an all-equity financed firm.

$$r_E = r_F + \beta_L\left(r_M - r_F\right)$$

and

$$r_0 = r_F + \beta_U\left(r_M - r_F\right)$$

Modigliani-Miller's final proposition says that although the shareholders demand a higher rate of return (offer lower prices) in the presence of debt, because of the lack of bankruptcy costs, the bondholders do not increase the level of returns they demand. The two exactly offset each other as debt increases, leaving the overall cost of capital untouched regardless of the debt level of the firm.

$$WACC = r_0 \qquad\qquad (4.5)$$

Again, this is easy to prove. We know the WACC is given by equation 4.1 and r_E is given by equation 4.3. Take equation 4.1, substitute the value of r_E from 4.3, and solve to give us equation 4.5.

$$WACC = r_D\frac{D}{V} + r_E\frac{E}{V}$$

$$WACC = r_D\frac{D}{V} + \left\{r_0 + \left(r_0 - r_D\right)\frac{D}{E}\right\}\frac{E}{V}$$

$$WACC = r_D\frac{D}{V} + r_0\frac{E}{V} + \left(r_0 - r_D\right)\frac{D}{V}$$

$$WACC = r_0\frac{E}{V} + r_0\frac{D}{V} = r_0$$

Let's translate this equation into more intuitive terms. Suppose you are running an unlevered firm with a current cost of equity capital (discount rate) of 10%. Your chief financial officer (CFO) comes to you and says that bondholders, being really nice people[7], are only demanding 6%. So as the CEO, you decide to repurchase half the firm's equity and issue debt instead. Are you better off?

Modigliani and Miller say no. While the bondholders do indeed demand 6%, because the risk increases, shareholders demand a lot more (the price goes down). How much more? Well, plugging in the numbers into equation 4.3 gives us

$$r_E = 10\% + (10\% - 6\%)\frac{1}{1} = 14\%$$

Unfortunately the average of 14% and 6% is still 10%. You get mad. These ungrateful shareholders are demanding higher returns, while the nice bondholders are still expecting 6%. You decide to get rid of more shareholders. Specifically, you go to 99.99% debt (leaving just 1 shareholder). What happens to the cost of equity capital? It goes up still further.

$$r_E = 10\% + (10\% - 6\%)\frac{99.99}{0.01} = 40006\%$$

But the overall cost of capital stays the same. What happens if you eliminate the last shareholder? You leave only the bondholders, right? Surely now, you have reduced the cost of capital? Again, no. What is a shareholder? A shareholder is someone who gets the residual income after everyone else has been paid off. Who gets it in this case given that there are no shareholders? The last persons remaining are now the bondholders, who are therefore just the shareholders by another name. So a 100% debt-financed firm is the same as a 100% equity-financed firm. And we know shareholders in a 100% equity-financed firm expect returns of 10%, which is what we started with.

You might note that all Modigliani-Miller's proofs depended almost entirely on the idea of no free lunch – if two items have the same payoff, they must have the same initial price; otherwise you have a free lunch.

So far, we have analyzed a perfect world. Now let us go on to add our first imperfection: taxes.

Capital Structure with Corporate Taxes

To begin, we define all the terms exactly as in the previous section. We have a levered firm with value V_L, an unlevered firm with value V_U, the same EBIT, borrowing rate, r_D, cost of equity capital, r_E, and the all other terms as before. We introduce one new term, corporate taxes, τ_C. These are taxes that the firm pays on its earnings after it pays interest. Effectively, what this implies is that the firm's cost of debt is lower than before. It pays r_D to its bondholders but gets back $\tau_C \times r_D$ from the government as a tax credit. Hence, its effective borrowing rate is $r_D(1 - \tau_C)$. The weighted average cost of capital, the WACC is then defined by

$$WACC = r_D\left(1 - \tau_C\right)\frac{D}{V} + r_E\frac{E}{V} \qquad (4.6)$$

As before, we need to answer the same three questions:

1. How does the value of the firm change when it levered up? Is V_L different from V_U?
2. How does the expected rate of return on equity, r_E change when the debt-equity ratio changes? In the absence of any debt, the expected rate of return on equity is r_0. Does this change when the firm levers up?
3. What happens to the firm's overall cost of capital, its WACC, as the firm levers up?

Modigliani and Miller's solution to these three questions was dramatically different from the answers in a perfect world. In a corporate tax world, their first proposition said that there is a tax advantage to choosing debt over equity. In fact, the value of the firm goes up with debt and is given by

$$V_L = V_U + \tau_C D \qquad (4.7)$$

Because interest on debt is tax deductible (interest is paid out before the profit is calculated and taxes are paid), paying interest reduces the firm's tax burden. Hence, there is more left over for the firm's shareholders. Recall that the bonds are always issued at zero NPV, so the bonds are just a tax avoidance device here.

Their second proposition said that although shareholders are still exposed to more risk than in the unlevered case, the shareholders are also partly shielded from the loss by the presence of a riskless tax shield. For that reason, while they still demand higher returns, they are willing to settle for returns that are lower than in the no-tax case. Finally, because the value of the firm goes up, this is reflected in the cost of capital. Since the cash flows stay the same, this means the firm's WACC goes down in the presence of debt and taxes.

Intuitively, let's again think of the firm as a giant pizza worth $10. Initially, you own the whole pizza. Unfortunately, because of taxes, you cannot consume the entire pizza. If the tax rate is 40%, you give the government a slice of pizza worth $4 and get only $6 worth of satisfaction. Think of the government like your neighborhood bully who grabs a portion of your lunch every day.[8] You know that the bully will not take any portion from the teacher's lunch. So before you come into school, you corner your teacher and sell him $4 worth of pizza. The teacher pays you $4, and you hide it (the bully won't notice cash, just pizza). Then when the bully asks you for 40% of your lunch, you give him $40\% \times 6 = \$2.40$ worth of pizza, leaving $3.60 for yourself. The amount you have is therefore $4 of cash and $3.60 of pizza for yourself, leaving you better off than before. In this case, you end up with $7.60. Of course, when we extend this to financial markets, shareholders are not really concealing the money. The key to remember is that interest payments are not taxed per se (they are paid out to lenders before taxes are paid), and that gives a benefit to the shareholders.

To see this more formally, consider investing in both the levered and unlevered firm. As before, let us buy 10% of the equity of the unlevered firm and 10% of the levered firm. Since the levered firm has both debt and equity, this means we buy 10% of the debt (bonds) and 10% of the equity of that firm. As before, since the market values of the two firms are V_U and V_L respectively, the costs of these two strategies are $0.1 \times V_U$ and $0.1 \times V_L$ ($= 0.1 \times E_L + 0.1 \times D_L$) respectively.

Both the firms' assets are identical. That means they both generate the exact same free cash flow, EBIT. But you need to pay taxes on the EBIT for the unlevered firm. The taxes are equal to $\tau_c \times$ EBIT. The remaining amount, $(1 - \tau_c) \times$ EBIT, goes to the shareholders. So in return to the investment of 10% of the equity of the unlevered firm, you get 10% of this free cash flow after paying taxes $= 0.1 \times (1 - \tau_c) \times$ EBIT.

For the levered firm, as before, the amount of interest is $r_D \times D_L$. As a bondholder, you own 10% of this stream. That means you get $0.1 \times r_D \times D_L$ as interest. The firm then pays taxes at rate τ_c on the remaining amount (EBIT $- r_D \times D_L$). The after-tax amount $(1 - \tau_c) \times$ (EBIT $- r_D \times D_L$) goes to the share-holders. But you own 10% of that stream as well. So you get $0.1 \times (1 - \tau_c) \times$ (EBIT $- r_D \times D_L$) as dividends.

Adding the two together, your total payoff is

$$0.1 \times r_D \times D_L + 0.1 \times (1 - \tau_C) \times (EBIT - r_D \times D_L)$$

Rearranging the terms gives us a payoff of

$$\{0.1 \times (1 - \tau_C) \times EBIT\} + \{0.1 \times \tau_C \times r_D \times D_L\}$$

The first term in this expression is exactly the same for the unlevered firm. The second term is new. It is the value of the annual tax shield $\tau_c \times r_D \times D_L$ multiplied by your proportional ownership of the firm.

But the value of the firm is the present value of all future cash flows to the firm. Here we need the present value of all future annual tax shields of the firm. Let's assume that the firm is in a steady state – it does not issue any new debt beyond the amount it already has. Let us also assume that the debt is per-petual: it has no maturity date. This is not an unreasonable type of debt; it is just another type of cash flow. We can value this as a perpetuity using equation 2.5.

What is the discount rate we use? You only get the tax shield if you can actually pay off the debt. Therefore, the tax shield is actually exactly as risky as the debt, and we can use the interest rate on the debt, r_D, as the appropriate discount rate.

Using the perpetuity formula in equation 2.5, the present value of the tax shield is

$$Tax\ shield = \frac{\tau_C \times r_D \times D_L}{r_D} = \tau_C \times D_L$$

Using this value lets us conclude that buying 10% of the levered firm makes us better off by $0.1 \times \tau_C \times D_L$. Therefore, by the no-arbitrage principle, the strategy of buying 10% of the unlevered firm must be exactly this amount more expensive than the strategy of buying 10% of the levered firm. In other words, $0.1 \times V_U + 0.1 \times \tau_C \times D_L = 0.1 \times V_L$ or $V_U + \tau_C \times D_L = V_L$, which is proposition 1. What is especially interesting is that the interest rate is still completely irrelevant to the proof, although the amount of debt now becomes important.

As before, let's put some numbers on this to make it easier. Suppose the firms both generate $100 of EBIT every year (small firms, remember?). Owning 10% of the equity of the unlevered firm costs $0.1 \times V_U$ and returns $6 as dividends after paying a 40% tax rate. There are no personal taxes, so the after-tax EBIT flows straight through to the shareholder. Owning 10% of the equity and 10% of the debt of the levered firm costs $0.1 \times E_L + 0.1 \times D_L = 0.1 \times V_L$. Suppose the levered firm has issued $100 of perpetual debt at a 10% interest rate. The firm generates $100 of EBIT and pays out $10 in the form of interest. The remaining $90 is subject to tax at 40%, so the shareholders only get the after-tax amount of $54 in the form of dividends. Since you own 10% of both streams, you get $1 of interest and $5.40 of dividends = $6.40, which is $0.40 more than before. Where is this extra amount coming from? It is the value of the tax shield given by the tax rate multiplied by the interest payment ($0.1 \times \tau_C \times r_D \times D_L = 0.1 \times 40\% \times 10\% \times 100 = 0.4$).

In the presence of taxes, Modigliani-Miller's second proposition says that risk to equity goes up in the presence of leverage, but because of the tax shield, the increase is not as much as before. The precise formula giving the return to equity is

$$r_E = r_0 + (r_0 - r_D)(1 - \tau_C)\frac{D}{E} \tag{4.8}$$

Let's prove this with an example. Start with an unlevered firm where the tax rate is 45%. Suppose the firm's annual EBIT is $200, its assets are worth $1,000, and since it has no debt, this is the value of equity as well. There are 1,000 shares giving us a stock price of $1. The ex ante expected return to this all equity financed firm is

$$r_0 = \frac{EBIT(1-\tau_c)}{Assets} = \frac{200(1-45\%)}{1,000} = 11\%$$

Now suppose the CEO announces that the firm will issue $500 of perpetual debt, paying 8% per year and uses the money to buy back shares.

Assuming market efficiency, the moment the firm announces the issue of debt, the market understands that what the firm is actually announcing is that it will issue a costless tax shield. According to Modigliani-Miller proposition 1 (equation 4.7), the value of the firm jumps instantly to $V_U + \tau_c D = 1,000 + 45\% \times 500 = 1,225$. This all happens at the announcement because the market is efficient – in such a market, since everyone is trying to make money ahead of everyone else, no one will actually wait for the debt to be issued. Everyone will buy the shares right away knowing that the value will go up on the issue date. So since there are still 1,000 shares outstanding, the stock price jumps from $1 to $1.225.

Now the firm actually executes the share repurchase. But it has issued only $500 of perpetual debt. This means it can buy back only 500/1.225 = 408 shares. What are we left with after the repurchase?

- EBIT = $200 (the assets of the firm have not changed)
- Interest = $40 (8% on $500 of debt)
- Assets = $1,225 ($1,000 of original assets + $225 from the tax shield)
- Debt = $500 (amount raised)
- Equity = $725
- Number of shares = 592
- Price per share = $1.225 ($725/592)
- Debt/equity ratio = 68.97% ($500/$725)
- EBIT – Interest = $160 ($200–$40)
- Tax = $72 (45% of $160)
- Cost of equity, r_E = 12.14% ($200 – $40 – $72 = $88 paid to $725 worth of equity)

The Modigliani-Miller formula (4.8) directly predicts this as below:

$$r_E = r_0 + (r_0 - r_D)(1 - \tau_c)\frac{D}{E} = 0.11 + (0.11 - 0.08)(1 - 0.45)\frac{500}{725} = 12.14\%$$

What would have happened in the no-tax case? In that case, when the firm announces an issue of debt, nothing happens to the stock price, since the firm value does not change (Modigliani-Miller no-tax proposition 1, equation 4.2). So the firm issues $500 worth of debt and buys back $500 worth of equity, leaving the debt-equity ratio = 1. Substituting in equation 4.3 gives us

$$r_E = r_0 + (r_0 - r_D)\frac{D}{E} = 0.11 + (0.11 - 0.08)\frac{500}{500} = 14\%$$

Hence, issuing debt also comes with a tax shield, which reduces the leverage effect.

Again, this can be expressed by the CAPM as well. Using a proof similar to the one used for equation 4.2, we have

$$\beta_L = \beta_U\left[1 + (1 - \tau_c)\frac{D}{E}\right] \qquad (4.9)$$

What happens to the firm's overall cost of capital, its WACC? Recall that the WACC is now given by equation 4.6 where we use the after-tax cost of debt in place of the original cost of debt.

$$WACC = r_D(1 - \tau_c)\frac{D}{V} + r_E\frac{E}{V}$$

However, as before, we can substitute the value of r_E from equation 4.8 to get

$$WACC = r_0\left(1 - \tau_c\frac{D}{V}\right) \qquad (4.10)$$

Equations 4.6 through 4.10 form the essence of capital structure theory in the presence of taxes. What they tell us is that in a world with efficient markets, symmetric information, and no bankruptcy costs, there are no disadvantages from borrowing and huge tax advantages from borrowing. So the pre-scription to any firm is to borrow as much as it can, ideally going to 99.9999% debt (the firm cannot go to 100% debt because that would be the same as an all-equity financed firm).

Unfortunately, taxes are paid not just by corporations but also by investors. In addition, investors may pay different rates on different types of income – capital gains, ordinary dividends, interest payments, and so on. Since investors can put off paying the capital gains tax till they sell their shares or even pass them on to heirs, tax-free, effective capital gains tax rates are usually lower than ordinary income tax rates. Moreover, investors may not hold the firms' shares directly but through a pension fund that is tax-free. Hence, the marginal investor, the investor who is likeliest to pay the highest price for a share, may be a tax-free entity that is not affected by personal taxes. Therefore, it is difficult to pin down exactly how personal taxes affect the firm's capital structure, and many economists do not even teach these concepts to business students.

More interesting is this question: If debt is so advantageous as a tax shield, why don't firms issue as much debt as possible? We rarely see firms with a 99% debt-equity ratio. Across the cross-section, many firms in fact have a pretty stable ratio. To explain why some firms have stable leverage ratios, we introduce the second major imperfection: bankruptcy costs.

The Trade-Off Hypothesis

There are two types of costs associated with bankruptcy: direct and indirect. Direct costs are costs that are relatively quantifi-able. For example, all sides have to pay legal fees, customers may cancel their orders for fear of a lack of service, suppliers may be reluctant to extend credit, and so on. All these factors, however, can be priced using the NPV framework. For example, a scenario analysis might be used to analyze the impact on a firm's cash flows when a supplier cuts off credit.

Indirect costs are much more difficult to quantify. The idea is that shareholders (who have control of the investment decision of the firm) can choose risky projects with negative NPV that will benefit them if the project pays off. Alternatively, they may choose to pass up safe projects with a positive NPV that benefit the bondholders instead of them. Finally, both managers and shareholders can choose to expropriate debt holders by paying themselves large payoffs and then declaring bankruptcy, leaving bondholders to pick up an empty shell. All three are examples of agency costs between the managers and shareholders on one side and the bondholders on the other. We will discuss more examples of agency costs in Chapter 6, on asymmetric information, but for now let's restrict ourselves to a couple of simple examples.

Suppose a firm is going into financial distress (though not yet bankrupt). Currently, its balance sheet looks like the one in Table 4.4.

On paper, the book value of the assets is unaffected by financial distress (the book value stays constant). However, the firm is producing products that no one wants to buy. Its fixed assets (machinery) are essentially worth nothing, since their output is so specialized that they cannot be used for anything else. So no one will buy even the machines, which means that their market value is effectively zero. What happens if the firm is liquidated today? The bondholders have priority. So they get whatever is left of the firm (essentially its cash worth $400), and the shareholders are left with nothing.

Now let us consider a project that is essentially a very risky gamble. It costs the firm $400 to invest in the project, which is all the firm's cash. There is a high probability (90%) that the project will be a complete failure, returning nothing. There is a 10% chance however, that the project will pay off big time with a potential cash flow of $5,000. Since the project is so risky, let's assume that its cost of capital is high, 45%. The expected cash

Table 4.4 Market value balance sheet for a firm in financial distress

Assets	Book value	Market value	Liabilities	Book value	Market value
Cash	$400	$400	Bonds	$600	$400
Fixed assets	$800	$0	Equity	$600	$0
Total	$1200	$400		$1200	$400

flow from the project is 5,000 × 10% + 0 × 90% = $500. Using the NPV formula (equation 2.1),

$$NPV = -400 + \frac{500}{1+0.45} = -55.17$$

Since the NPV is negative, our conclusion from Chapter 2 would have been to reject the project since the benefits do not outweigh the costs. However, the wrinkle here is that the shareholders are making the choice using someone else's money (the bondholders') to make the decision. From the point of view of the bondholders, this is a very bad decision. Without the project, they would at least get the cash in the firm ($400). With the project, they only have a 10% chance (if the project pays off) of getting the face value of their debt back ($600) and a 90% chance of getting back nothing at all, for a total expected value of $60. In present value terms, again using the NPV formula, this is worth much less than $400:

$$NPV = \frac{60}{1+0.45} = 41.38$$

The shareholders, however, have every incentive to take the project. Without taking the project, their expected payoff is zero. If they take the project, there is a 10% chance that they will get a payoff of $5,000, pay off the bondholders, and get a final dividend of 5,000 − 600 = 4,400. There is a 90% chance that the project will fail, in which case they get zero, but then they would have got zero anyway if the project had not been taken.

So with the project, they get an expected payoff of 4,400 × 10% + 0 × 90% = $440. Again using the NPV formula, this is worth

$$NPV = \frac{440}{1+0.45} = 303.45$$

So in the presence of financial distress, shareholders have incentives to overinvest in risky projects with negative NPVs. But this is not the only incentive the shareholders have. They also have an incentive to underinvest in safe projects with positive NPV.

Consider a government contract that gives the firm a guarantee of $600 one period from now. This is risk-free, so the required rate of return is 10%. However, to deliver the contract, the firm will have to make an investment of $500. Using the NPV formula,

$$NPV = -500 + \frac{600}{1 + 0.10} = 45.45$$

Given that the firm has only $400 worth of cash now, the firm has to raise $100 from somewhere. Will the shareholders invest the additional $100? It turns out the answer is no. Without the project, the shareholders have an expected value of zero. If the project is implemented, the firm gets a cash flow of $600 one period from now, and all of it will go to pay off of the bondholders, leaving the shareholders with nothing, even though they have had to reach into their pockets to pull out an additional $100. We don't even have to use the NPV formula to see that the shareholders will refuse to accept this project, even though the NPV is positive.

A third possibility is very straightforward. Whether or not any new project appears, the shareholders have an incentive to pay themselves a large dividend of $400, and declare bankruptcy leaving the bondholders with nothing. Similarly, managers can increase the perquisites they pay themselves when the firm is going into distress.[9]

What this means is that the potential cost of financial distress increases as the firm accumulates more and more debt. The trade-off hypothesis argues that firms trade off the benefits of debt (tax shields) against the cost of debt (financial distress costs), leaving an optimal amount of debt each firm should have. Unfortunately, financial economists don't have a clear answer about how much the actual value of financial distress cost varies with the level of debt, so we wave our hands a bit and say that firms figure this out through trial and error. If we ask managers whether they do have a target debt ratio in mind when deciding to issue debt, a large proportion will say that they do, although they can't really tell you how they came up with that number. Overall, all we can say is that the optimal amount of debt is (roughly) given by Figure 4.1.

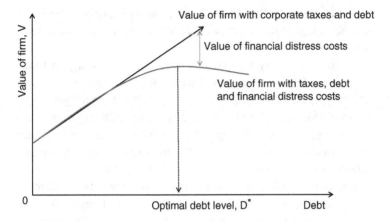

Figure 4.1 The optimal amount of debt in the presence of taxes and bankruptcy costs

The trade-off hypothesis meshes well with some observations on firm debt policy. For example, it explains why high-tech industries (with a lot of intangible assets) use relatively little debt. It also explains why airlines (with a lot of tangible assets) use a relatively large amount of debt. It explains what types of firms are candidates for leveraged buyouts. Leveraged buyouts are transactions where the buyer issues a huge amount of debt to buy the firm. Prime candidates for LBOs are firms with lots of assets and very stable cash flows (firms with low financial distress costs). It explains why firms with lots of debt make paying off that debt a priority – they sell assets and stop dividends. Unfortunately, there are a number of observations that are left unexplained. For example, a number of very successful profitable companies have very little debt. Their financial distress costs are low. Why then do these firms pass up the chance of creating value through a debt tax shield? To answer this question, we turn to an alternative model of capital structure – the pecking order hypothesis. This approach is based on asymmetric information.

The Pecking Order Hypothesis

The pecking order hypothesis is named after the pecking order displayed by chickens on a farm. Apparently, chickens, like many social animals, work out a social hierarchy that governs the order in which they feed, drink, crow, mate, or dust bathe.[10] Chickens higher up in the pecking order feed before chickens lower in the pecking order.

In finance theory, the pecking order hypothesis argues that the cost of financing increases with the differences in the level of asymmetric information possessed by inside managers to outside investors. There are three types of financing available to managers: retained earnings, debt, and equity. Debt and equity both involve the managers going to the market to raise capital. When do insiders have the most asymmetric information relative to outsiders? In the case of debt, outsiders just need to worry about whether the firm will pay its interest payments and whether it will pay off its face value eventually. In other words, all they have to do is answer questions on its solvency. In the case of equity, not only do they need to decide questions on solvency, they also need to decide questions on whether the firm will deliver on its growth opportunities. These growth opportunities are particularly difficult to value for outsiders. Financial statements are not very helpful in deciding what the value of these opportunities may be, since the managers may have not have made the decisions yet (and may never choose to do so) to take advantage of these opportunities.

Managers, however, are unlikely to tell investors the true value of the opportunities. They always have incentives to tell investors that the opportunities are worth enormous amounts, even though in reality, they may not be worth very much at all. Rational investors therefore discount the claims of managers and mark down the value of equity every time the manager issues equity.

To see this through an example, consider a firm where the manager knows that the true value of the firm including its growth opportunities is $100 per share. Since the market has considerably less information than the managers, investors sometimes believe that the shares are worth $150. In this case, a manager who wishes to raise capital should definitely issue equity. She gets $150 for a piece of paper that in reality is worth $100. The manager would not be acting in the interests of the long-term shareholders of the firm if she did not issue equity. In contrast, suppose investors believe that the shares of the firm are actually worth $80. The manager should not issue equity since she gets $80 for a share that is actually worth $100. Hence, in this case, the manager will issue debt, not equity.

Outside investors do not see all these calculations made by managers. All they know is that if the manager issues equity, the firm is likely to be overvalued while if the manager issues debt, the firm is not likely to be overvalued. Consequently, an equity announcement is bad news, and investors will mark down the price of existing shares in the firm if the manager issues equity.

These observations imply a pecking order in financing for firms. Since the firm does not face asymmetric information issues with retained earnings, it first chooses to finance its investments with retained earnings. If retained earnings are not enough, it prefers debt as its next choice, since there is considerably less disagreement on what debt is actually worth. If debt is not enough, the firm finally chooses to raise equity as a last resort.

The pecking order hypothesis explains why many profitable firms do not issue debt. They do not have to since their retained earnings are enough to cover their investments.

There have been additional stories[11] put forward to explain why firms issue debt at some times and shift to equity at other times, or to explain the capital structure of firms. Some of these stories appeal to market irrationality. For example, they assume that the market develops preferences for equity at some times and managers cater to these preferences by issuing debt when the market shifts away from equity and they issue equity when the market shifts to an equity preference. Some attribute them to managerial preferences. For example, managers who were born in tough times (like the great depression or who lived through traumatic times while growing up) are less likely to issue debt when they are at the helms of firms.

What is the bottom line? Not very much, unfortunately. We can tell you some stories about what kinds of firms have particular types of structures, we can tell you why some firms do not have structures of the type we predict for them, we can explain some differences in capital structure across industries, we can show that firms behave as though they had a target debt-to-equity ratio, and we can show that changes in leverage change firm value in predictable ways when firms lever up or lever down, but we don't really know much beyond that. In a way, this is not all that surprising. The concept of financial distress and the actions firms take to prevent this are all endogenous. In other words, many firm actions are determined simultaneously. We are not in the position of physicists who can change one variable while holding all others constant to determine the incremental impact of that change on the whole. Financial economists are also not always able to draw reliable and replicable conclusions from counterfactuals.

Let's leave this painful topic for a bit and go back to a throwaway comment I made earlier in this section, when I said that growth opportunities are particularly difficult for outsiders to value. How is the value of a growth opportunity measured anyway? Some growth opportunities are easier to value than others. For example, valuing a straightforward project means computing its cash flows[12], its discount rate (as in Chapter 3), and adjusting that discount rate for the presence of debt (as in this chapter). But some projects are contingent on other events happening first. For example, a firm might start a pilot plant to test-market a new product. It will choose to expand this pilot plant into a full-fledged factory only if the product is successful. If it is unsuccessful, the firm abandons the pilot plant.

Here the managers have not yet made the investment decision for the full factory (and may never choose to do so) to take advantage of these opportunities. The investment decision is implemented only if the test marketing is successful. We can compute the NPV of the pilot plant, and we can compute the NPV of the full factory. But how do we calculate the value of the option to build the factory *only* if the pilot is successful? Surely it depends on the probability that the pilot is successful? But where do we get this probability from? Consider Apple coming out with its first Apple iPad, for example. What were the chances that this device would be successful? This was a brand-new product unlike any other in the industry at the time. No one could calculate these probabilities.

To figure out how to value these contingent opportunities, we turn to the next major idea in finance: option pricing.

Notes

1. The genius behind all the ideas in finance so far involves some kind of decoupling decision. For example, the concept of NPV allows managers to decouple the investor's investment preferences from the firm's investment decision, and the concept of portfolio theory allows managers to ignore investors' levels of risk aversion and focus only on their portfolio holding decision.
2. Even the workers and executives are clones.
3. Since we assume that markets are efficient and competitive, if the pizza gave you more than $10 worth of satisfaction, the pizza seller is undercharging you and will go out of business being replaced by more efficient contractors. If the pizza gives you less than $10 worth of satisfaction, you will never buy a pizza from that place again, and competition being what it is, the pizza place will again be driven out of business.
4. Apologies to any lawyers who may be reading this book.
5. If you choose not to pay up, that is not a problem except that you will own less of the unlevered firm (7% to be precise).
6. Suppose you don't need to borrow it. You have the money lying around. Will this change your final payoff? Won't you be better off? No, because economists say you will be ignoring the opportunity costs. If you did not give the money to the firm, you could have invested it at 20%. By giving it to the firm, you are missing out on the 20%, which is the same as saying you are borrowing at 20%.
7. This is hypothetical. There are no nice people in finance.
8. In the United States, Republican party members/readers may find this analogy more convincing than Democratic readers.
9. Bondholders are not idiots, however. In many cases, they can anticipate the shareholders' incentives, and so they usually insist on the presence of covenants that prevent the shareholders from paying extraordinary dividends or selling senior debt. They are also more reluctant to lend to firms coming close to distress.
10. I say *apparently*, because not being raised on a farm, I have no idea whether this is indeed true. Perhaps this is one of those apocryphal stories like milk actually coming from animals called cows instead of from hygienic packs in the supermarket. In any case, this is a textbook on finance, not animal husbandry.
11. I call them stories because they are all on the vague side. You might want to think of them as parables or analogies, rather than precise and testable hypotheses.
12. As we noted in Chapter 2, the cash flows generated by the firm are its free cash flows (FCF) defined as after-tax EBIT + depreciation – capital expenditure – increases in working capital.

5 Option Pricing Theory

Learning Points

- ■ An intuitive explanation of derivative securities
- ■ Forwards and futures
- ■ Options
- ■ The binomial model
- ■ The Black-Scholes model
- ■ Real options

An Intuitive Explanation of Derivative Securities

Every summer in Cambridge, England, the Cambridge Shakespeare Festival puts on a series of plays in the college gardens. These are very popular with the audience, who bring their own chairs, blankets[1], and picnic baskets to watch Shakespeare in a gorgeous college garden. However, there is one big downside – the English weather. Buying the (non-refundable) tickets well in advance will reserve a place for you but, unfortunately, exposes you to the risk that it will pour down on the day of the performance, leaving you sitting on a sodden blanket[2] watching a bunch of unhappy actors who would also rather be elsewhere. Not buying the tickets in advance, in contrast, exposes you to the risk that the weather will be gorgeous on the day but the show will be sold out (or that ticket prices rise too much for you to afford), leaving you on the road outside the garden, listening to the sounds of merriment and wishing you were inside.

One way out might be to monitor the weather forecasts religiously and buy the tickets as soon as you realize that the weather is going to be good. But there are two problems with this solution. First, nearly everyone is doing this, so you still don't have a guarantee that you will be first to the ticket office when the forecast is a clear evening. Second, weather forecasts in England are notoriously unreliable, so if you are depending on the weather bureau[3] to accurately estimate probabilities of rain more than a day out, you are incurably optimistic.[4]

What is the best thing to do? You could call the ticket box office and ask for a call option[5] on the ticket.[6] Specifically, you would ask to reserve the tickets. But you would reserve them in a special way. What you would tell the box office is that you want to place the tickets on hold. If it does not rain, you would pick up the tickets right before the show and pay (say) the current price of £15. If it rains however, you would pass up on the event and not show up, paying nothing for the ticket. This would be the ideal arrangement for you since you have no risk left. In good weather, you get the ticket, and in bad weather, you stay in a warm comfortable pub, chortling at the thought of the non-finance types who were silly enough to buy the tickets well in advance.[7]

Unfortunately, what is good news for you is not good news for the box office. If everyone bought these kinds of reserved tickets, the box office would only get the price for the tickets in case of good weather. It couldn't charge more than the pre-agreed price. It wouldn't even have the right to refuse to sell the ticket to you.[8] In bad weather, it would be stuck with a bunch of unsold tickets (or returned tickets if it sold put options) but still bear all the fixed costs of putting on the show.

You might think that the box office would have no interest in selling you these kinds of tickets. In fact, a lot of them already do, but you may not recognize them clearly as options. For example, consider top Michelin-starred restaurants. A number of them keep your credit card on file. If you do not cancel at least three days ahead of your reservation, you are charged a substantial non-refundable booking fee. That is the cost of the option you are buying to keep a reservation at the restaurant open. Similarly, fully refundable hotel rooms that can be cancelled at any time up to twenty-four hours before checking in are more expensive than nonrefundable hotel rooms. The difference between the two rates is the value of the option to cancel. Award airline tickets bought with loyalty or frequent flyer benefits are typically refundable (on the payment of a nonrefundable fee). The fee is the cost of the option to cancel the reservation. All these are options.

And if you want the option to cancel a Shakespeare ticket, the box office will charge you a fee to compensate it for the risk it bears.

So how does the box office price the reservation fee? It can't charge too high an amount because if it does, no one will pay it and people may go to other plays put on by rival companies that charge lower fees. It can't charge too low an amount because if it does, it will go bankrupt when too many people exercise the option to cancel and no one shows up for the show. So it needs to get the price just right. How does it do this?

You may imagine that it depends on the box office estimating how likely it is that it will rain. But remember, this is England. No one has any idea how likely it is that it will rain.[9]

So what do you do? This was the problem academics were faced with when they were coming up with an option pricing theory. The problem appeared insurmountable because no one knew how to compute the probabilities. The answer that Fischer Black, Myron Scholes, and Robert Merton came up with was simple and ingenious. The probabilities were already built into the underlying asset. In our case, the underlying asset was the ticket to the play. As people update their probabilities to whether it will rain on the day, the ticket becomes more or less valuable.

But how does the box office know when the ticket is becoming more or less valuable? Don't they have to check the weather themselves? One way out would be to check the prices on a secondary market such as Stubhub. If the rain is expected to hold off, you might see the tickets selling for higher prices on Stubhub. If it looks much more likely to rain, the prices on Stubhub are more likely to crash. The idea is that the hundreds of people trading tickets on the secondary market have much better information and incentives to monitor the weather than one meteorological office in the computer. But can even a crowd predict the weather successfully?[10]

So if even the secondary market cannot predict the weather, how can we price the option? Black, Scholes, and Merton realized that it is possible to construct a portfolio consisting of the underlying asset (the actual ticket) and a government riskless bond. This portfolio has the same final payoff as the option. Hence, by the no-arbitrage idea, it must also have the same initial cost as the option. That means that we do not ever have to worry about the probabilities or what people think about the probabilities. Does this method of proof sound familiar? Yep, it is the same proof as we used for capital structure. Because of this insight, Scholes and Merton received the Nobel prize in 1997. In the rest of this chapter, we will derive the value of the option to cancel using this basic approach.

Incidentally, options have been around for several thousand years. How did people price them before we came up with the formal option pricing formula? Surprisingly well, it turns out. The option values derived from historical data accord very well with the formula from our modern pricing formulae. This may perhaps be due to an argument involving the survival of the fittest.[11] If you consistently misprice options, you will go bankrupt very quickly. So, although you may not know how the option is priced, you would know a set of values for which you would not go bankrupt. You would price as though you knew the formula.

Forwards and Futures

Let's start with the simplest type of derivative instrument: a forward. A forward transaction is a trade where a price and an execution date are set today, but the trade is actually carried out not today but on the execution date, which is sometime in the future. Let's apply this to the box office example.

In Cambridge, the box office is far away from the college gardens, and you need an actual paper ticket to get into the gardens. Suppose you can physically go to the box office, buy a paper ticket today for a show a year from now for £15, and take the ticket home. We refer to this as the spot price. Alternatively, you can call the box office today, reserve a ticket and provide your credit card details. The ticket is nonrefundable, so your card will be charged. Unfortunately, you are close to your credit card limit, so you would like to pay for the ticket only on the day of the show, when you actually have money in your account.

The box office tells you that it will be happy to charge you when you actually pick up the ticket on the day of the show. But £15 today is not the same as £15 one year from today. How much should it tell you the price will be on that day? We'll call this the forward price.

In all cases, I am going to assume that there is an active secondary market and a large number of buyers and sellers for Shakespeare plays in the college gardens. I am also going to assume that the box office will change the price of the ticket according to demand (like a plane ticket). Finally, the box office is not sold out – there are always tickets that can be bought straight from the office. These assumptions allow us to set bounds on the competitive price that can be charged, abstracting away from complications such as scarcity or bargaining power.

I am also going to assume that the annual risk-free rate (the rate on government bonds, see Chapter 2) at the time is 1%. In this case, the price the box office should charge you is £15.15.

To understand why, suppose the box office says it will charge you £16 when you pick up the ticket. Then you can make money. Borrow £15 at the risk-free government rate, and buy the ticket (pick it up today), and offer to sell it to anyone who would like to pay the amount on the show day for less than £16 and more than £15.15. If you charge £15.50 for example, buyers will come to you rather than to the box office. On the day of the show, the buyer pays you £15.50, you give her the ticket, and repay your loan of £15. With 1% interest, you repay £15.15, making a profit of £0.35.

Similarly, suppose the box office says that you will have to pay £15.10 on show day to pick up the ticket and suppose you already have a ticket. Then, you sell your ticket at the spot price today £15 and reserve a ticket at the box office for £15.10. What do you do with the £15 today? Invest it in government bonds of course. That fetches you £15.15 after interest on show day, use £15.10 to buy the ticket, netting you a profit of £0.05.

Hence, the only price at which neither you nor the box office can consistently make money is £15.15. This is the no-arbitrage price and is also the price of the forward. In general terms, if S is the spot price, the price of a forward contract is given by:

$$F = S \times (1 + r)^t \tag{5.1}$$

It should be easy to recognize this formula. It is precisely the future value of a single lump sum formula in Chapter 2 (equation 2.3). Similarly, if we use continuous compounding (equation 2.7), the price of a forward contract is

$$F = S \times e^{rt} \tag{5.2}$$

Using this equation, the price of the forward contract is £15.15075, almost the same but not quite.[12]

Notice that it does not cost you anything to enter into a forward contract. This is because the contract is really not reducing risk. It is shifting the direction of risk. By buying a forward ticket, you are protecting yourself against the risk of the ticket being sold out on the day of the show. But you are still not protected against the risk of rain. You are still obliged to go through with the transaction on the contract as traded. So if it is raining, the secondary market price of the ticket may be £1, but you are still obliged to pay £15.15, the price you originally contracted on. The box office benefits because you pay the full price for a ticket that is trading at £1. Of course, if it is bright sunny weather, the box office could have raised the price of the ticket to £30, but it is still charging you £15.15, causing it to lose out. The takeaway is that a forward contract does not reduce risk in the sense that it does not reduce the variability of the outcomes that you face. It flips the type of risk you take. Previously you were worried that the ticket would be sold out before the show if you did not buy early. Now you are worried about the weather.

The risk involved with these contracts is illustrated by the cautionary tale of the economist John Maynard Keynes, who was appointed First Bursar[13] of King's College in Cambridge in 1924, a position he kept till his death. Keynes bought several forward[14] contracts on wheat in 1936. As the maturity date approached, Keynes became increasingly concerned about the price of wheat, which was going down instead of up as he had predicted. Keynes had quite a large bet on the value of wheat, having purchased forward about one month's supply of wheat for the whole country. Many commodity contracts do not actually involve delivery of the underlying commodity but Keynes, reluctant to take a large loss and no doubt hoping to wait and hold pending a price recovery, measured up the size of King's College Chapel during the weekend and thought he could take physical delivery of about half the wheat.[15]

But there is another problem. Let us suppose that you have bought a forward contract on your ticket for £15.15. But now the weather prospects are horrendous, so the ticket price is only £1. You have strong incentives to renege. In other words, you disappear, changing your address and cancelling your credit card. This means that without the two parties monitoring each other, one of the two parties has the temptation of refusing to go through with its side of the deal. The need for continuous monitoring makes it difficult to expand the forward market significantly.

The forward market developed two features that made it explode in popularity. One was the development of standardized contracts. For example, if you bought a contract on wheat, it could not be any old wheat, it had to be graded on a standardized system (in the U.S. wheat future, for example, it had to be one of Spring, White Winter, or Red Winter), it was traded in particular amounts (lots of 1,000 or 5,000 bushels, for example), and it was delivered in particular months of the year. The seller was given the choice of deciding on the day or grade of delivery and could tender the wheat on any day between the first and last day of the month of maturity. In the Shakespeare ticket market, that might mean a ticket in the front row, with four seats in the center row, no more than 12 feet from the stage.

What standardization means is that I can now sell my forward contract to anyone else in the secondary market without any confusion as to what I am selling. The secondary market buyer does not need to know the type of ticket or any special arrangements I have made with the box office. He or she need never even contact the box office.

The second was a system of marking to market. Both buyers and sellers open accounts at the clearing house facilitating the trade. At the end of every day, the old contract is valued at the market price prevailing at the time, and the profits and losses are assigned to each party. Then a new contract is written with the prices fixed at the end of the previous day.

For example, take the forward contract for the Shakespeare ticket at a price of £15.15. At the end of the day, a significant number of people think the weather is going to be worse than expected. So the spot price drops to £14. What this means is that you have made a paper loss. You had contracted to buy a ticket, now worth £14, at £15.15, a paper loss of £1.15. The box office has made a corresponding profit of £1.15. The clearing house transfers £1.15 from your account (called a margin account) to the box office's account and writes you both a new contract at £14. So now you have lost £1.15 and have a new contract to purchase a ticket at £14 364 days from today. Tomorrow, if the price of the ticket goes up to £16, the clearing house takes £2 from the box office's account, puts it in your account, and writes you both a new contract at £16. You and the box office are required to maintain a minimum amount in your respective accounts. If you fall below this maintenance margin, you are required to top up your account.

Why this cumbersome process? The assumption is that the price of the ticket will not drop by a huge amount on any one day. Hence, both parties minimize the risk that the counter-party will default. Also, since the amounts, times, and quality of the product are standardized, there is little disagreement on what the terms of the contract involve. Hence, trading these standardized forward contracts, now called futures contracts, has become a huge multi-trillion dollar business, with futures bought and sold on organized exchanges. In many cases, when the contract is closed out, the physical product is never even delivered. For example, if you speculated on Shakespeare ticket futures, you could buy a future on a ticket today at £15.15. You could close out your deal two days from now when the price rises to £16, netting you a profit. Also, the box office does not have to be involved. You could buy a contract from a friend on tickets sold by the box office. As long as the secondary market is active, the box office is irrelevant here.

Does the mark-to-market feature mean that forward and futures prices are different? No, it turns out that they can be taken to be the same when the maturity and asset prices are the same and interest rates are independent of the asset price. They can be a little different when interest rates are positively or negatively correlated with the asset price.

There are some variations possible when applying equation 5.2. For example, suppose the asset provides a known income during the life of the contract, as in a utility stock that pays regular dividends. In this case, the forward price is given by

$$F = (S{-}I) \times e^{rT}$$

where I is the present value of the dividends that are expected to be received during the life of the contract.

Similarly, suppose the asset provides a known yield during the life of the contract, as in a stock index that pays not actual dividends but a regular yield. In this case, the forward price is given by

$$F = \frac{S}{e^{qt}} \times e^{rt} = S \times e^{(r-q)t}$$

where q is the average yield that is expected to be received during the life of the contract. Another example of an asset that provides a known yield is a foreign currency. Here the yield is the foreign risk-free rate. Hence, the forward price is

$$F = S \times e^{(r-r_f)t}$$

where r_f is the foreign risk-free interest rate. Finally, we need a variation for consumption assets where there may be storage costs (as in wheat or oil forwards) but also a convenience yield. If I have a forward contract to buy oil a year from now, that is all very well, but if I unexpectedly need the oil two months from now, the forward contract won't really help me very much. So there is a cost of having the contract instead of the physical product, and we call this cost the convenience yield. Putting these two costs in one by one, if the storage cost per unit time (as a percentage of the asset value) is u, then

$$F = S \times e^{(r+u)t}$$

since u is a cost, not a benefit. We don't really know how to measure convenience yields, so we actually start with the forward price F and the spot price S. Then rolling all the other costs (storage cost, interest cost, and any intermediate income earned) into a total cost of carry, c, we have

$$F = S \times e^{(c-y)t}$$

where *y* is the convenience yield.

It is important to note that every single variation has a formula that is derived from equation 5.2, which in turn is derived from equation 2.7 (in turn derived from our fundamental equation 2.3). Overall, as I have said before, we go a long way in finance with very few tools.

Options

Now, though forwards are very easy to value, they don't reduce risk. To reduce risk, you need an option. An option is the special reservation we discussed at the beginning of this chapter, which involves buying the ticket at a price we set today (what we will call the exercise price) and picking it up on the day of the show (what we call the exercise date) only if it does not rain. To value this option, I am going to start by deriving some boundaries on its price. In many cases, we will not be able to get an exact price for the option, but the price must always be within the bounds we establish here. I need to set up some technical jargon here to make it easier to refer to. I'm going to bold-face the jargon items to make them easier to refer back to.

The **option price** (also called the option premium) is the price we are paying to set up our reservation. Buying the option means that we are paying a price to the ticket office now in order to reserve our ticket. We will refer to this reservation, specifically an option to buy something, as a **call** option. Similarly, if we wanted an option to sell something, we would ask for a **put** option. **Exercising** the option means actually going to the box office, paying the exercise price, and picking up the paper ticket.

Let us denote the price of the underlying ticket today as S_0 (the zero standing for date zero, today). At current prices, $S_0 = £15$. The price of the ticket will fluctuate randomly depending on the weather and demand. So let us denote the (unpredictable) future price of the ticket by S_t. The amount of fluctuation is measured by the ticket's volatility, σ. Let the exercise price of the ticket (the price you fix today for which you will buy the ticket) be K. K need not be equal to S_0. You could get an option to buy the ticket for, say, £20. This is obviously less risky for the ticket office than letting you buy it for £15, so the ticket office would charge a lower price for that option. Or you could buy a more valuable option to buy the ticket on the exercise date for £10. Let us assume to make it general, that you want a valuable option, the right to buy the ticket for £10 even though it is currently selling for £15.

The risk-free rate, r_f, is the rate on government T-bills. Let us assume that this is 1% per year. The time to expiration, T, is obviously the day of the show (no point in getting a ticket you can only buy after the show is over), one year from today.

There are two types of reservations. The first type is an option that we can only exercise on the day of the show. We will call this a **European option**. The second type is an option that we can exercise any time before the show begins whether tomorrow or three weeks from today. This is called an **American option**.[16] Since an American option with the same parameters as the European option offers all the same benefits plus the option to exercise early (you can exercise on the day of the show as well as any time before), the American option is always worth at least as much as the European option and is sometimes worth more. If we denote an American call option by the term C, and a European call option by the term c[17], then we can write

$$C \geq c$$

Similarly, the value of an American put option would be worth more than that of a European put option

$$P \geq p$$

With all this jargon at our fingertips, let us now derive the bounds for a European call option. The first bound, of course, is that the call option can never be worth more than the underlying ticket. In other words,

$$c \leq S_0$$

This is kind of obvious. If the right to buy something is worth more than actually buying the item, why not just buy it? There is no downside (I'm assuming that the item is not something illegal, of course). So in our case,

$$c \leq 15$$

However, the call option must be worth more than the current ticket price less the present value of the exercise price.

$$c \geq S_0 - Ke^{-rT} \qquad (5.3)$$

In our case,

$$c \geq 15 - 10e^{-0.01} = 15 - 9.82 = 5.18$$

If we bought the option to buy the ticket at £15, this would change the formula to

$$c \geq 15 - 15e^{-0.01} = £0.27$$

Wait, what about the right to buy the ticket at £25? This would make the lower bound on the value of a call

$$c \geq 15 - 25e^{-0.01} = -£9.55$$

That is true but also a little bit worthless, since an option can never be worth less than zero. So the actual lower bound is zero or $S_0 - Ke^{-rT}$, whichever is higher. But how do we get this formula anyway? Well, like most of the other proofs we have, we do this by applying the no-free-lunch idea. Let us set up two portfolios as in Table 5.1.

Equation 5.3 says that c must be greater than £15 – £9.82 = £5.18.

To prove this, let us suppose it is not. Specifically, suppose c is selling for £5 today. That means that portfolio 1 is cheaper than the equation predicts. Now one of the fundamental principles of making money on the stock market is easy: buy cheap

Table 5.1 Portfolio costs and payoffs

Portfolio	Asset	Value	Value today in our example	Value on expiration date
1	A call option	c	c	Depends on ticket price
	An amount of cash equal to the present value of the exercise price	Ke^{-rt}	£9.82	£10
2	The ticket	S_0	£15	S_T

and sell dear.[18] Portfolio 2 is relatively more expensive than 1 according to the equation, so sell the ticket and buy portfolio 1.[19] Selling short the ticket gives us £15 today. Use £5 to buy the call, and deposit the remaining amount in a risk-less government bond yielding 1% per year. At the end of one year, on the show day, you have $10e^{0.01} = £10.10$ in your account.

Suppose the ticket is selling for £18 on show day. You would exercise the option, pay the exercise price (£10) and pick up the ticket. You can then return the ticket to the person you originally borrowed the ticket from, making a small profit of £0.10.

Suppose the ticket is selling for £9 on show day. Throw away the option, since it is worthless. Use the money in your account to buy the ticket on the open market for £9 and return it to your lender, leaving you £10.10 − £9 = £1.10 as a profit.

What this says is that for any option price less than £5.18, you can always make a completely riskless profit. Since there is no free lunch in finance, prices less than £5.18 are not possible.

This may seem a little esoteric, but it can be used to show that you would never exercise an American option early if the underlying asset pays no dividends. Suppose you own an American option on the ticket, allowing you to exercise it early. Suppose today the ticket is selling at £12 (so the option to buy at £10 is still valuable) and there is still one year to go for show day. Equation 5.3 tells us that the option cannot sell for less than $12 - 10e^{-0.01} = £2.09$. Suppose you receive private secret information that a giant storm will hit Cambridge on the day of the show. If everyone knew this information, the price of the ticket would plummet. You might think that a good thing to do is to exercise the option, pay £10 to pick up the ticket and sell it immediately for £12. Unfortunately, that would net you only £2. The option itself is worth at least £2.09. So instead of exercising, you would be better off selling the option. What this means is that there is no value to exercising an American call option on a non-dividend-paying stock early. Hence, in this special case:

$$C = c$$

Similar bounds can be established for European and American puts. The proof is similar. Set up two portfolios and show that if the price of the put is outside the bounds, it is possible to make money risklessly. Since this is prohibited in finance, the price of the option cannot fall outside those bounds.

So how do we set up the portfolios? Well, it is easiest to think of the problem as follows: A call option gives me the right to buy an asset. For that, I need money. So one portfolio will always consist of the call and the present value of the exercise price. Similarly, a put option gives me the right to sell an asset. But to do that, I need the asset. So the put option and asset go together in the other portfolio. In our example above, we had the call option and the present value of the exercise price in one portfolio and the ticket in one portfolio.

We can use precisely this idea to come up with the relationship between call and put prices in Table 5.2. On the day of the show, let us suppose the ticket price is £20. Then in portfolio 1, you exercise the option and buy the ticket using the amount in your bank account for £10. So you are left with a ticket worth £20. In portfolio 2, the right to sell the ticket at £10 is worthless if the ticket is selling on the open market for £20. So we throw away the option and are left with the ticket worth £20. Both portfolios are worth the same.

Similarly, let us suppose the ticket price is £8. In portfolio 1, you throw away the option and are left with £10 in your bank account. In portfolio 2, you exercise the right to sell the ticket for £10 and are left with the exercise price worth £10. Again both portfolios are worth the same.

Table 5.2 Constructing equivalent portfolios to illustrate put-call parity

Portfolio	Asset	Value	Value today in our example	Value on expiration date
1	A call option to buy at £10	c	c	Depends on ticket price
	An amount of cash equal to the present value of the exercise price	Ke^{-rt}	£9.82	£10
2	The ticket	S_0	£15	S_T
	A put option to sell at £10	p	p	Depends on ticket price

Since the values of the two portfolios are the same regardless of what the ticket value is on show day, the initial costs must be the same. Therefore, we can write

$$c + Ke^{-rT} = p + S_0 \qquad (5.4)$$

This equation is termed **put-call parity**. All it means is that option prices are related to each other and we can derive any type of derivative from the prices of other derivatives.

The Binomial Model

We are going to use that one basic idea (no free lunch) and the same basic methodology to derive the value of a simple call option on a Shakespeare ticket. As before, there are three instruments we can use: the ticket, an option on the ticket, and the exercise price (which is risklessly invested in government bonds). Let's keep all the parameters the same from the previous sections. In other words, you can buy the ticket today for £15. The exercise price is £10. The riskless interest rate is 1%, and time to show day is one year.

The binomial model to value options is so called because it assumes that the price of the ticket can only change to one of two numbers on the exercise date. It can rise to £25 (if the weather is sunny and the demand is high), or it can drop to £5 (if the weather is rainy and demand is low).[20] This is illustrated in Figure 5.1. The figure illustrates both the evolution of the

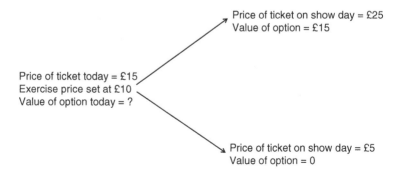

Price of ticket today = £15
Exercise price set at £10
Value of option today = ?

Price of ticket on show day = £25
Value of option = £15

Price of ticket on show day = £5
Value of option = 0

Figure 5.1 A one-stage binomial model of ticket prices

ticket price and the corresponding option value on the show day. If the ticket is worth £25 on show day, the option to buy it at £10 is worth £15 on that day. If the ticket is worth £5, the option is worth nothing.

There are three ways to compute the value of the call option using a binomial tree. The first approach is to create a combination of the ticket and the option that is riskless (that is, it is like the government bond investment). Second, we can use special probabilities called risk-neutral probabilities. Third, you can create a combination of the ticket and the riskless bond that replicates the option. Each of these has its own particular advantages and disadvantages. Let us start with the first approach.

Here we have a combination of the ticket and the option that should give you the same riskless payoff regardless of the value of the share on the exercise date. Recall that we don't place the call option (the right to buy the ticket) and the ticket into the same portfolio (no point in buying the right to buy something you already own). So let us sell someone else the call option instead. The buyer now has the right to buy the ticket from you at the exercise price of £10. As the seller, you don't have any rights – if the buyer wants to exercise, you have to sell him or her the ticket at the pre-agreed exercise price. But you need something to give if the buyer wants to exercise the option, so that is the ticket. So your portfolio consists of the price obtained by selling one call option, c, and the cost of buying a number of tickets currently worth £15 each. How many tickets precisely? Well, we have to work that out. For now, let's say we buy Δ (the uppercase Greek letter) tickets, Δ being the number we have to calculate.[21]

So, the current cost of the portfolio is £15Δ – c.

On the exercise date (show day), suppose the ticket has gone to £25. The value of the ticket part of your portfolio will go to £25Δ. But the option buyer will definitely exercise his or her option and buy the ticket for £10. That costs you £15. So your show day payoff is £25Δ – 15.

Now take the other side. Suppose the ticket has gone to £5. The value of the ticket part of the portfolio is £5Δ. The option is valueless, so the option buyer will throw it away leaving you off the hook.

In order for this to be riskless, the two payoffs must be exactly the same. Therefore, we have

$$£25\Delta - 15 = £5\Delta$$
$$£20\Delta = 15$$
$$\Delta = 15 / 20 = 0.75$$

So if you bought 75% of a ticket, you would not care whether the ticket price went up or down.[22] But what is the actual value of your portfolio? Substituting $\Delta = 0.75$, the value of the portfolio on show day is either $25 \times 0.75 - 15$ or $5 \times 0.75 = £3.75$. But what is the value of the portfolio today? Well, we know that it is given by $15\Delta - c$. But if $\Delta = 0.75$, this is equal to $11.25 - c$. We also know that the value on show day is a riskless 3.75. So the value today is the value of the portfolio on show day discounted at the riskless rate for one year, which is $3.75 \times e^{-0.01} = £3.71$. So $£11.25 - c = £3.71$, which implies that $c = £7.54$. According to equation 5.3, the call option cannot be worth less than $S_0 - Ke^{-rt}$, which is $15 - 10e^{-0.01} = £5.10$, so this fits the bounds perfectly.

What is interesting here is that we did not need to know anything about probabilities at all. It did not matter to us whether the ticket went up or down and the probability that it did so. All that mattered was setting up a suitable portfolio to completely get rid of all risk.

The second approach, the **risk-neutral probability approach**, relies precisely on this implication. The idea is that if we do not need probabilities, any probability will do. In particular, the probabilities assigned by one certain type of investor will do. This investor is a very special investor in that he or she does not actually exist in real life. The investor is risk neutral. In other words, if he or she is asked to choose between getting £100 for sure or a coin toss that pays off £200 if the coin comes down heads and zero if it comes down tails, the investor will be indifferent. The expected value of the coin toss is still $200 \times 1/2 + 0 \times 1/2 = 100$, but there is a 50% chance we never get anything. In reality, most of us would definitely prefer a sure thing to a random gamble with the same expected value, but only a 50% chance of winning.

But as we have already noted in the first approach, probabilities don't matter, so we can pretend that the risk-neutral probabilities estimated by the risk-neutral investor are just as good as anyone else's. Let us suppose that the risk-neutral probability of an up movement is p and obviously the risk-neutral probability of a down movement is 1– p.

Then the risk-neutral investor would not care either getting the ticket for sure for £15 or getting a chance of a ticket worth either £25 or £5. What is the expected value of this ticket? It is given by $25 \times p + 5 \times (1 - p)$. But this is the value next period. What is the value today? Since the investor is risk neutral, the right discount rate to use is again the riskless rate. So we have $15 = (25 \times p + 5 \times (1 - p))e^{-0.01}$. Solving for p gives us p = 50.75%, which means that $1 - p$ = 49.25%.

The call option is worth £15 if the ticket goes to £25 and worth zero if the ticket goes to £5. So the expected value of the option using risk-neutral probabilities is £15 × 50.75% + £0 × 49.25% = £7.61. The value of this today using the riskless discount rate is £7.61$e^{-0.01}$ = £7.54, which is exactly the same as the first method.

Why on earth did we even bother with this alternate method? Well, as we noted earlier, assuming the ticket price can go to only one of two values, 25 or 5, is silly. In reality, the ticket price can go to 15, 25, any number in between or above. It can't go below zero, but that is the only restriction. So how do we handle this? We expand the binomial tree. Figure 5.2 shows a tree with two steps, each step occurring once every six months. Here the ticket prices can take on one of three values (here £41.67, £8.33, or £1.67). The interest rate still stays the same, but over six months, the value is half its previous value. This is a little more realistic but not much more.

If we use the first approach, we need to start at the ends of the tree and work backwards, computing Δ every time. That is a pain in the posterior (though we will do it in the third method that follows). However as long as the tree is symmetrical (it goes up and down in the same proportion every time), the risk-neutral probabilities will stay the same every time. These proportions by which the tree goes up or down are called the up and down factors respectively. In our case, the up factor is 1.67 (25/15 = 1.67), and

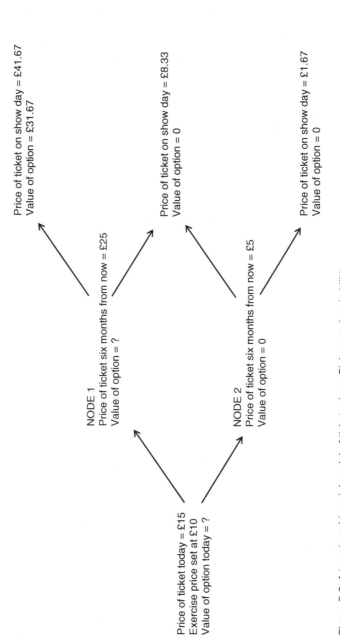

Price of ticket on show day = £41.67
Value of option = £31.67

Price of ticket six months from now = £25
Value of option = ?

NODE 1

Price of ticket on show day = £8.33
Value of option = 0

Price of ticket today = £15
Exercise price set at £10
Value of option today = ?

Price of ticket six months from now = £5
Value of option = 0

NODE 2

Price of ticket on show day = £1.67
Value of option = 0

Figure 5.2 A two-stage binomial model of ticket prices: Risk-neutral probabilities

the down factor is 0.33 (5/15 = 0.33). Do these factors stay the same? Yes, (after rounding off) 25 × 1.67 = 41.67, 25 × 0.33 = 8.33, 5 × 1.67 = 8.33, and 5 × 0.33 = 1.67.

But since the first step is the same as before, we can compute the risk-neutral probabilities exactly as before:

$$15 = (25 \times p + 5 \times (1 - p))e^{-0.01 \times 0.05}$$

The only difference between this and the previous case is the time period is for six months (half a year instead of one year). Solving for p gives us the risk-neutral probabilities as 50.376% and 49.624% respectively. So the value of a call at the upper node 1 is (50.376% × 31.67 + 49.624% × 0) $e^{-0.01 \times 0.5}$ = £15.87. At node 2, the value of the option is zero since the values of the options at both end points are zero. Therefore, the value of the option at the beginning is (50.376% × 15.87 + 49.624% × 0) $e^{-0.01 \times 0.5}$ = £7.95. The value is pretty close to the previous value.

So as we create finer partitions over shorter and shorter time periods[23], we get a more and more complex binomial tree. But the beauty of the risk-neutral probability approach is that we do not need to keep on recalculating the values of the ticket. Once we have the up and down factors, we can mechanically program this into a computer, which will churn through the tree for us and spit out the option value at the end.

The two methodologies so far allow the box office to price an option. Now, suppose the box office feels that this is a service it would rather not offer. In other words, there are no special reserved tickets available anywhere. Are we done for? Actually not. In the third approach, called **dynamic hedging**, we can artificially create an option that hedges our risk completely. All we need to do is trade the ticket and the riskless bond appropriately. Fair warning – this is going to be a tedious process. It requires the existence of an active secondary market where the tickets are traded, such as Stubhub.

To understand how this works, let us start with Figure 5.2 again, but this time we are going to replicate the payoffs to the option using the ticket and the government bond. This is illustrated in Figure 5.3.

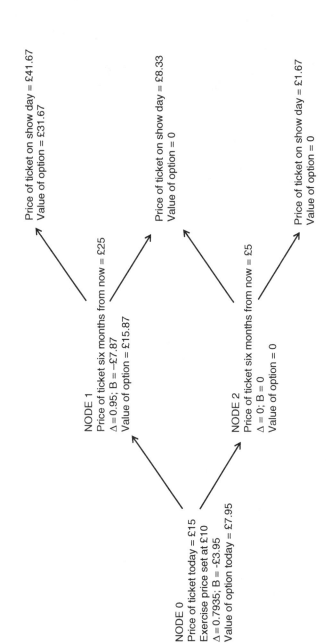

NODE 0
Price of ticket today = £15
Exercise price set at £10
Δ = 0.7935; B = –£3.95
Value of option today = £7.95

NODE 1
Price of ticket six months from now = £25
Δ = 0.95; B = –£7.87
Value of option = £15.87

NODE 2
Price of ticket six months from now = £5
Δ = 0; B = 0
Value of option = 0

Price of ticket on show day = £41.67
Value of option = £31.67

Price of ticket on show day = £8.33
Value of option = 0

Price of ticket on show day = £1.67
Value of option = 0

Figure 5.3 A two-stage binomial model of ticket prices: Dynamic hedging

Let us create a portfolio consisting of buying Δ tickets and borrowing an amount, B. The value of this portfolio must be given by Price of the ticket $\times \Delta - B$.

At node 1, the ticket price can either go up or down. If it goes up, the value of the option in the second period must be given by 31.67. If it goes down, the option is worth nothing. These two values must also be the value of the portfolio. So we have two equations with two unknowns:

$$41.67\Delta + Be^{0.01 \times 0.5} = 31.67$$
$$8.33\Delta + Be^{0.01 \times 0.5} = 0$$

Solving these two gives us $\Delta = 0.95$ and B = −£7.87. The negative value of B means that we are investing a negative amount in the government bond. Or to put it another way, we are borrowing £7.87 at the government bond interest rate. At node 1, therefore, the value of the option is 15.87, exactly the same as in approach 2:

$$25\Delta + B = 15.87$$

At node 2, we have

$$8.33\,\Delta + Be^{0.01 \times 0.5} = 0$$
$$1.67\,\Delta + Be^{0.01 \times 0.5} = 0$$

which means that both Δ and B = 0 and the value of the option = 0 as before.

Now go back to the initial node 0. Using the same steps, we have

$$25\,\Delta + Be^{0.01 \times 0.5} = 15.87$$
$$5\,\Delta + Be^{0.01 \times 0.5} = 0$$

which implies that $\Delta = 0.7935$ and B = −£3.95. At node 0, the value of the option is

$$15\Delta + B = £7.95$$

So the values have not changed from the risk-neutral approach 2. Why then did we use this complicated approach?

That is because we can now use these values to create an artificial option. Let us start at node 0. At node 0, we know that $\Delta = 0.7935$ and $B = -£3.95$. So first we buy 0.7935 tickets and borrow £3.95. If the ticket price drops to £5, the tickets are worth $5 \times 0.7935 = £3.97$. However, we now owe $£3.95e^{0.01 \times 0.5} = £3.97$. The net value of the portfolio is zero, as is the value of the option, and the portfolio is liquidated.

If the ticket price rises to £25, the value of the ticket part of the portfolio rises to $25 \times 0.7935 = £19.8375$. But the new Δ is 0.95. So an additional $0.95 - 0.7935 = 0.156$ tickets must be purchased. Where do we get the money from? By borrowing an additional $25 \times 0.156 = £3.91$. By now our original borrowing has grown to £3.97, so we owe a total of £7.88. The value of the overall portfolio is $0.95 \times 25 - 7.88 = £15.87$, which is exactly the value of the option on the tree.

From node 1, the ticket can rise to £41.67 or drop to £8.33. If it drops, the value of the tickets is given by $8.33 \times 0.95 = £7.92$. We now owe $7.88e^{0.01 \times 0.5} = £7.92$, so again the portfolio is worthless (as is the option) and can be liquidated. If the ticket rises to £41.67, the value of the tickets is given by $41.67 \times 0.95 = £39.58$, while we continue to owe £7.92. The value of the portfolio is therefore £31.67, which is the value of the option at the top node.

What this (complicated) procedure shows is that it is really unnecessary to have someone create an option. If an option is not being sold, and you would like to really hedge all your risk, you could create a dynamic hedge that precisely replicated the option value at every point in time. If the asset price went up, you would buy more of it and borrow to finance your purchase. If the price went down, you would sell a portion of your holdings and get rid of some of your borrowing.

This is also the basic idea behind **portfolio insurance**. Portfolio insurance involved creating artificial hedging strategies that would exactly insure the value of a portfolio. However, they were also blamed for exacerbating financial crises. Recall that what these strategies do is hedge after movements in prices. If the price goes up, they buy more. If the price goes down, they sell. What that means is that if there is a market panic with prices crashing, automated portfolio insurance strategies that

The Black-Scholes Model   **121**

involve selling in the same direction as the market can make the collapse deeper. They were in fact partly blamed for the October 1987 collapse in prices worldwide.

The Black-Scholes Model

The binomial tree approach is very intuitive in explaining how options work. However, it is also cumbersome to use. Black, Scholes, and Merton made a number of assumptions about how stock prices evolved. In particular, they assumed that stock prices follow a random walk[24], and percentage changes in the stock price in very short intervals of time are normally distributed.[25] They assumed that there were no transaction costs or taxes and that all securities were perfectly divisible. This assumption allows us to trade as many times as we want in our dynamic trading strategy without incurring costs. The perfect divisibility assumption allows us to trade fractions of a ticket. They assumed that the stock did not pay dividends during the life span of the option. They also assumed no riskless arbitrage (no free lunch), continuous trading of securities (in instantaneous time), a constant riskless short-term rate of interest, and finally that investors could borrow and lend at the same riskless rate of investment.

Some of these assumptions have since been relaxed, but the idea is still straightforward. It involves setting up a riskless portfolio consisting of a position in the derivative and a position in the stock. Given the no-arbitrage assumption, the return from the portfolio must be the risk-free interest rate. If this is the case, then the other assumptions described above mean that a particular differential equation[26] can be set up to model the way the stock price evolves. The Black-Scholes formula is a solution to that differential equation. Actually, it is one of a family of solutions. Which solution is the right one depends on the boundary conditions we apply. Boundary conditions just tell us what the value of the option will be at the boundaries of the stock price and the time of expiration. For example, the boundary condition for a European option is that the value of the option at the expiration date must be max(S−K,0).

Applying this boundary condition to the particular differential equation that Black and Scholes used to define the evolution of the stock price, the price of a call option on a non–dividend-paying stock is given by

$$c = SN(d_1) - Ke^{-rt}N(d_2)$$

where

$$d_1 = \frac{\ln(S_0 / K) + (r + \sigma^2 / 2)T}{\sigma\sqrt{T}}$$

and

$$d_2 = \frac{\ln(S_0 / K) + (r - \sigma^2 / 2)T}{\sigma\sqrt{T}} = d_1 - \sigma\sqrt{T}$$

where

c = European call option price
S = current stock price
K = current exercise price
r = riskless interest rate
t = time to maturity
σ = volatility

Though the Black-Scholes formula looks complicated, applying it is ridiculously easy. Many traders in fact, treat it as a Black box[27], inputting the five ingredients, S, K, r, t, and σ into a suitably programmed calculator and writing down the output on the other side.

Real Options

Option pricing can be used for far more than just valuing securities, however. A huge number of corporate investment decisions can only be modeled using option theory. For example, consider a firm that wants to introduce a new model of a smart phone. The problem is, of course, that there are several models of phones out there already with heavy competition among the firms. While the firm's model is new and innovative, it has no idea whether this model will be accepted by consumers. But it does not need to build a billion-dollar factory right away. It can start with a pilot plant. The pilot plant allows it to make a few phones for a small amount of money and see how they do. If they do well, the firm can then expand the plant into a major operation. This is an option to expand. The firm does not have to expand. It chooses to do so only if the product is successful. Similarly, the firm may have an opportunity to abandon the project if it is not successful. This is also valuable.

To illustrate a real option through an example, consider a manager of a fashion store who is considering building an outlet in a new and upcoming area in the city. Suppose the manager is offered a long-term lease on a prime property in the area. However, it is by no means guaranteed that the area will generate enough foot traffic from tourists to justify opening the outlet. The manager can ask for a get-out clause in the lease. If, in two years, say, the foot traffic has not increased to the point when the outlet is successful, the manager can break the lease at no cost. This get-out clause is an option, and adding it to the contract will increase the value of the deal to the manager. How much the manager has to concede on the other terms of the deal to get the get-out clause can serve to estimate the value of the option.

Though real options are potentially incredibly useful, they also suffer from a big weakness. Recall that the methods we used to value the option involved setting up a riskless hedge with the underlying security and a risk-free government bond. However, sadly in the case of real options, the underlying asset is often very infrequently traded, if at all. That is why in the case of the Shakespeare tickets, we had to assume the existence of an active secondary market. Without the market, we could not really have created a riskless hedge, and hence we would not have been able to price the option. In the fashion outlet example above, we would need stores to be actively traded, so that we can compute the volatility, σ. But they are not. This creates a huge limitation of real options. Though theoretically they are incredibly valuable, practically they are difficult to value.

Overall, however, derivatives have been one of the most successful types of financial instruments ever created. Their basic principles of valuation are exactly similar to the principles used to discuss the value of capital structure in Chapter 4 – no arbitrage. To value a derivative, the idea is always to replicate the payoffs to the derivative by creating an artificial portfolio whose value we do know and then deriving the price of the option from the price of the portfolio.

Notes

1. It can get cold even on a summer evening in Cambridge.
2. If you were a true-blue financial economist, you might abandon the tickets as a sunk cost. If you were a more normal human being, you might choose to sit, shiver, and curse the weather gods.
3. The Met Office in the UK.
4. Or, as we say in finance, irrational.
5. A more general word for any kind of option is a derivative, since the prices are derived from the price of the underlying asset, in our case, the ticket.
6. Actually, you would not do this, since the box office salespeople are unlikely to have finance degrees and would just think you were nuts.
7. Or you could actually pay for and pick up the paper ticket today but simultaneously buy a put option on the ticket, the right to sell it back to the box office at say the current price of £15 only if it rains.
8. The seller of the option has no rights but all the obligations. If the buyer wants to exercise the option, the seller *will* be disadvantaged but will *have* to go through with the deal, which is why the seller charges the buyer for the right to buy.
9. The correct answer ranges from very likely to almost certainly.
10. The answer is that they can't. At least not in Britain.
11. Financial economists love arguments involving the survival of the fittest, though we would almost certainly lose any argument if it came down to surviving a zombie apocalypse, for example.
12. See note 17 in Chapter 2.
13. An English term for the treasurer of the college.
14. Technically futures contracts (see following discussion for the distinction).
15. Fortunately, this did not prove necessary since the price of wheat did go up eventually, and Keynes ended up making a small profit.
16. You might guess that American options are so called because Americans are sometimes perceived to be notoriously demanding and self-indulgent, requiring immediate gratification. But you would be wrong. These are just conventions for the type of option. The name has no relation to the options' geographic or behavioral characteristics. Sometimes an American option is just an American option.
17. By saying that the capitalized C is an American option, while the small c is European, I acknowledge that in English, a capital letter is not necessarily more valuable than a small letter. This is again a matter of convention. I am not being a capitalist.

18. And in an another application of the fundamental rules of finance, that piece of free advice (which is guaranteed to make money) is worth precisely … nothing. No free lunch.

19. How can you sell a ticket if you don't actually have it? In finance, that is not a problem. What we do is borrow the ticket, sell it (a process called selling short), and return the ticket to the lender on show day. There are, of course, minor complications such as how does the lender trust you to return the ticket, but there are also lots of institutional features and safeguards to minimize the risk (margin accounts and other features discussed in the previous section).

20. Is this realistic? Obviously not. But bear with me while I start complicating stuff.

21. Finance people love throwing around Greek terms casually. They know it is all Greek to other people.

22. Just a moment, you'll be saying at this point, how can I buy 75% of a ticket? You can't. So just multiply everything by 100 which means that you sell 100 options and buy 75 tickets.

23. Instead of once every six months, consider the possibility of the price changing every second, or every micro-second and doing so over the course of the entire year

24. A random walk is a mathematical construct that describes a path consisting of a series of random steps. For example, random walks have been used to model the path traced by a molecule in a gas.

25. Economists love normal distributions.

26. The equation was a version of the heat equation in physics that has very well-known solutions.

27. Pun not necessarily intended.

6 Asymmetric Information

Learning Points

- The lemons problem
- Agency problems
- Signaling models
- Screening models
- Corporate governance

So far, information has not really played much of a role in deriving all the basic ideas in finance that we have encountered so far (net present value, portfolio theory, capital structure, and option pricing). However, assumptions on information underlie many of these ideas. Specifically, most of the ideas that we have derived have been based on the assumption of symmetric information – everyone has the same information to value the asset. However, this is not a very realistic assumption. In the last two chapters in this book, we explicitly turn to the role information plays in setting prices for transactions. In this chapter, we are going to allow for the possibility that the buyer and seller of any asset have different information regarding the true value of an asset. In this case, who is better off?

The Lemons Problem

Typically when we think of assets, we think more is better: a person with a larger house is better off than a person with a smaller house, more money is better than less money, and so on. Interestingly, *information* is the one asset where possessing more does not necessarily leave you better off. This insight earned George Akerlof, along with his colleagues, Michael Spence and Joseph Stiglitz, a Nobel Prize in 2001.

We take it for granted that we do not have all the information we need to evaluate any purchase we make. For example, if we buy a phone, will the phone run apps we download a year from now? Will the new phone be comfortable in our hand when we make calls, or will it be easy to share photos of our exploits with our admiring friends? Will committing to a particular operating system lock us into that system for future purchases? These are all issues we might consider when deciding what phone to buy.[1]

We also take it for granted that when making a deal, we have more or less information than the person on the other side of the deal. For example, if we are buying a used car, we have less information than the seller. If we are renting a house, we have less information than our future landlady about problems with the house: whether it leaks in winter, whether there is mold in the house, and so on. But the landlady also knows little about us as potential future tenants. Will we keep in the house in good order? Do we have little monsters who will rampage through the house destroying the furnishings and keeping the house in a mess? These types of information asymmetry will affect how much we are willing to pay to rent the house or buy the car. They will affect whether the landlady is willing to be flexible on the rent in order to get us as tenants. How exactly is the information incorporated into the prices we pay?

Let us start with an example of buying a used car. We may have a maximum figure in mind when we set out to buy a car. Economists call that figure our willingness-to-pay (WTP) price. Similarly, the seller has a figure in mind when deciding the minimum price she is willing to accept for the car. We call that number the seller's willingness-to-accept (WTA) price. Suppose we are willing to pay £3,000 for a used car in good condition. If the seller is willing to accept £2,500 for the same car, we have the makings of a potential deal. According to economists, any price between £2,500 and £3,000 is a good deal, what economists call an efficient outcome. For example, if we settle for a price of £2,700, both of us are better off. The seller gets £200 more than her minimum, and we get the car for £300 less than our maximum. The difference between the WTP price and WTA price is called the economic surplus, and a lot of economic theory analyzes the division of the economic surplus between buyer and seller.

Much of the division depends on the relative bargaining power between the buyer and seller. For example, if there is a large demand for used cars and few sellers, the sellers have a lot of bargaining power. They will extract almost all the surplus as the buyers will be buying at the top end of their price range. Similarly, if there is a large supply of used cars and few buyers, prices will drop to the bottom of the economic surplus range. Akerlof's insight was to show that if there is enough asymmetric information in the market between buyers and sellers, there are situations when good deals (in which there is an economic surplus) will still not happen – the buyers would only be willing to pay less than the minimum the sellers would accept. In an extreme situation, even in the presence of good deals, the market breaks down completely.

To show why this problem happens, Akerlof came up with an example he called the "lemons problem." Suppose there are two types of used cars on the second-hand car market – good cars (which I will call plums) and lemons. Plums are great cars – they require little maintenance and never break down. Lemons are prone to breaking down frequently and require a lot of maintenance. Buyers would be willing to buy lemons, but they just would not want to pay the same amount for a lemon as they would for a plum. To put numbers on this, let us suppose that buyers would be willing to pay £3,000 for a plum and £2,000 for a lemon. For simplicity, assume that buyers and sellers are homogenous – they all have the same WTP and WTA respectively. Sellers, in contrast, would be willing to sell a plum for £2,500 and a lemon for £1,500. This means that every deal has an economic surplus of £500 (£3,000 – £2,500 or £2,000 – £1,500) and therefore if deals are done, they are economically efficient.

Let us suppose that the market has many more buyers than sellers. This gives more bargaining power to the sellers. The example also works if we assume more sellers than buyers, though here, of course, the bargaining power is higher for buyers.

Start with the case of symmetric information. If both buyers and sellers can differentiate a plum from a lemon perfectly, when will the market clear? Every car will be sold. The plums will all sell for £3,000, and the lemons will all sell for £2,000. The economic surplus goes to the sellers since they are few in number relative to the buyers. If a buyer balks at paying less than the maximum WTP, the seller can reject him easily knowing that another buyer will come along shortly.

Now let us suppose that the seller knows perfectly which car is a plum and which is a lemon since she has been driving the car for some time. However, buyers can no longer differentiate a plum from a lemon. All the buyer knows is what he has read in the local newspapers where historical statistics are recorded. The buyer knows that on average, in that area, 70% of the cars are lemons and 30% are plums. What price should the rational buyer offer? The only rational price is a weighted average of the two WTPs which is 30% × 3,000 + 70% × 2,000 = £2,300.

Offering less than this, say £2,000, would lead to someone else coming in and offering more and getting a small probability of buying a plum for the price of a lemon, a possibility which is worth *something*. If the buyer offered £2,300 however, who would accept? Definitely not the sellers of the plums – they know their cars are worth at least £2,500 to them. So they would not sell if the price offered was less than £2,500. That means the only sellers willing to transact would be lemon sellers. But a rational buyer would anticipate that and hence would only offer £2,000 for what is guaranteed to be a lemon.

Who is worse off in this example? Definitely not the buyers, that is, the parties with less information. They know that they will only be offered lemons at £2,000, but that is the price that they are willing to pay for a lemon. Definitely not the lemon sellers – they are willing to sell their cars for £1,500 and are receiving £2,000 for them. The only people who are worse off are the plum sellers. If they could persuade the buyers that they are selling good cars, then they would be able to get £3,000, but given the absence of any credible persuasion method, they withdraw from the market.

There are two lessons to be drawn from this example. First, asymmetric information hurts the sellers with more information *and* superior products. Second, the equilibrium in this example is fully revealing. In simpler terms, even though the seller might say nothing about the quality of the car, the fact that she is willing to transact tells buyers instantly that she is selling a lemon. In economics, we call this a *separating equilibrium* – the plum sellers are separated from the lemon sellers. There are two more lessons that are better understood after we encounter a slightly different example.[2,3]

In this variant, suppose that historical data reveals that 30% of the cars typically sold in the past are lemons and 70% are plums. What price should the rational buyer offer? Similar to the previous case, the only rational price is a weighted average of the two WTPs which is 70% × £3,000 + 30% × £2,000 = £2,700. If the buyer offered £2,700, who would accept now? Unfortunately, both types of sellers would accept, making the equilibrium price less than fully revealing. In economics, we call this a *pooling equilibrium* – the plum sellers are pooled with the lemon sellers into a common pool where everyone sells their car for the same price.

Again, who would care? The buyer would not, because he has some probability of paying a high price for a lemon but has a larger probability of getting a plum cheaply. The lemon sellers love the idea of getting £2,700 for the lemon, so they actually benefit from the presence of asymmetric information. The only sellers who hate the asymmetric information are the plum sellers who get the average price of £2,700 instead of the true price of £3,000.

Again, the first lesson is exactly the same as before – asymmetric information hurts sellers with more information and superior products. But what are the two new lessons? The first is that the superior sellers are motivated to spend some money in order to persuade buyers that they are selling plums. In this example, we can even put a precise value on this amount. Plum sellers will not be willing to spend more than £300 to persuade a buyer that they have a good car. Why not? Because identifying themselves as a plum seller nets them £3,000, but pooling with the lemon sellers nets them £2,700.

But why spend any money at all? That is because if the plum sellers successfully separate from the lemon sellers, the lemon sellers get £2,000 for their cars. Hence, if they can find a way to imitate the plum sellers and increase the asymmetry of information, they will.

The second new lesson says that sellers with inferior products will try to copy the sellers with superior products whenever they can. Hence, superior sellers will never be able to persuade a buyer just by telling the buyers that they have superior products – because the lemon sellers will tell the buyers exactly the same thing.

Because cheap talk will be copied instantly by the lemon sellers, the persuasion tactics that plum sellers use will therefore have to be costly – but not too costly.

Agency Problems

For asymmetric information to be a problem, there have to be at least two parties with different levels of information. A self-sufficient farmer – living by himself, growing all his own food, and making his own clothes – will not need to worry about asymmetric information, since he does everything himself. But, the moment he employs a farm hand, asymmetric information problems begin because both parties have information the other does not. For example, the farmer knows precisely how difficult the farm is to manage. But the farm hand knows precisely how much he is willing to work.

This is a situation that economists call a *principal-agent problem*. The principal is someone who hires an agent to do some work for him. For example, on the farm, the farmer is the principal, and the farm hand is the agent. If you would like to sell your house, you are the principal, and the agent is the real estate agent.

Principal-agent problems only arise in the presence of asymmetric information and take one of two guises. The first is the issue of selecting the right agent to do the work, called the *adverse selection* problem. The second is the issue of making sure that once selected, the agent does not shirk on the job, a problem called the *moral hazard* problem.

To get an intuitive sense of what these two issues are, consider one of the most famous (fictional) agents of all time: James Bond. James Bond is hired by M., the head of the British Secret Intelligence Service (also known as MI6). We know that Bond has a double zero designation, which gives him a license to kill. But how was Bond selected in the first place? Sadly, the movies only lavish attention on Bond's adventures *after* he joined MI6, giving almost no detail on the procedures an organization such as MI6 would have in place to first select a OO agent, let alone control him once he is on the job.

Consider the problems a government department would have in selecting OO agents. These agents would have to be willing to kill on behalf of their country *and* be willing to do this on a government paycheck. He (or she) should not be willing to kill for any other reason. Now, placing an ad in the newspaper for someone who is willing to kill for her country, might indeed attract a candidate who fits the ideal requirement of a patriotic psychopath who is willing to work for a government salary.[4] However, it is equally possible to attract a candidate like Hannibal Lecter. That is the adverse selection problem.

Suppose a carefully designed ad really works: It successfully attracts the ideal candidate. Is MI6's problem over? The answer is no. The next problem is to make sure that the candidate is willing to work equally hard after being selected. But this is extremely difficult. The candidate is being paid a government salary, which is really not very high. On assignment, however, the candidate gets to stay in the Four Seasons hotel, empty the minibar, seduce beautiful spies, and in general live an exotic and thrilling life. Suppose M., worrying about the government budget, calls James Bond and asks him the status of his current assignment. M. would like Bond to finish his assignment as quickly as possible and return to England. Bond, however, likes living an exotic life, and therefore has an incentive to exaggerate the difficulty of the assignment. What would he tell M.? He might say, for example, that the assignment is really difficult, security around the target is really tight, and he needs much more time to carry it out (all the while staying at the Four Seasons). He might also ask for a bigger operating budget (including a larger minibar tab) and more exotic toys to play with. Unfortunately, since Bond is the expert at the scene, M. has no idea whether Bond is actually justified in making these requests. This is the moral hazard problem.

So how do we solve these two problems? Economists talk about two different ways in which these problems can be solved. In the first approach, the party with more information takes the action. These are signaling models. In the second approach, the party with less information takes the action. These are screening models.

Signaling Models

In a signaling model, the party with more information takes an action to reveal its type. As an example, let's go back to the car sale case. Recall that the sellers with their superior information *and* superior products were the one who were disadvantaged. In particular, in the second example, the plum sellers would have been willing to pay up to £300 in order to distinguish themselves from the lemon sellers. What kind of signals would they be able to use?

One possibility might be to offer insurance to the buyer for the first year. If the insurance costs less than £300, the plum seller would be able to persuade the buyer that he would indeed be selling a good car. Similarly, another option might be to tell the buyer to bring his own mechanic and that the seller would be willing to pay for the cost of this due diligence. In both these cases, the signal would only work if the lemon seller would not be able to copy the plum seller and similarly offer to pay for a mechanic (knowing for example, that no mechanic would be able to find all the problems with the car).

Let us take a more precise example to pin this down. The classic example used by many economists is the labor market. Let us suppose that there are two types of workers: good and poor. Each worker knows whether he or she is a good worker, but there is no way for prospective employers to determine which type a particular worker is. In particular, every worker would say that he or she is good.

Let us assume that good workers are worth £160,000 to the firm while poor workers are worth only £100,000. Good workers have an outside option of taking a job in some other industry for £110,000, while for poor workers, this alternative pays only £70,000. Note that working in the other industry is not the preferred option for either type of worker. It is their worst-case scenario.

Suppose that half the workers are good and half are poor. In addition, suppose that workers are in short supply so that competition among employers drives up the market wage up to the true value of the employee. First, let us suppose that information is symmetric. This means that both the workers and their employers know who is a good worker and who is a poor worker. The employers will then offer £160,000 to the good workers, and they will offer £100,000 to the poor workers. If information is asymmetric, the employer will offer ½ × 160,000 + ½ × 100,000 = £130,000 to all their workers. Again, as in the car sale case, the employer is indifferent. Sometimes (50% of the time) they will get a shirker for £130,000, but 50% of the time, they get a hard worker for the same salary. The poor workers love the asymmetric information. They get a much higher salary than they would get had they been identified as a shirker. Again, the only ones hurt are the hard workers.

So the hard workers have incentives to show that they are hard workers. They need signals. What is an appropriate signal for the labor market? There are two characteristics for the ideal signal. The signal must be costly. In addition, for the good workers, the benefit of sending the signal must be greater than its cost, while for the poor workers, the cost must be greater than the benefit (so that they don't copy the signal). One possible signal is education.

Suppose (perhaps hypothetically) that students learn nothing in business school that contributes to their productivity. What would the value of education be? It is not quite zero, as you might be thinking. This is because getting into a prestigious business school itself has a value as a signal.

Assume that for £50,000, a good worker can apply to, attend, and graduate from a prestigious business school. A poor worker, inherently less intelligent and motivated, must spend an extra £20,000 (on prep courses to get admitted, on tutors while in school, and psychic costs of working twice as hard, etc.) in order to acquire the same degree. What is the benefit to a worker in obtaining a degree?

Suppose a good worker indeed spends the money to get a business degree. Let us also suppose that the signal is credible. In other words, if an employer sees a worker with a degree, the employer automatically assumes the worker is a good worker and pays her £160,000. For a good worker, the degree costs her £50,000 for a total first year salary of £110,000. In contrast, the degree costs a poor worker £70,000 for a final first-year take home of £90,000. Will the poor worker get the degree? The answer is no. The worker is better off not getting the degree, hence identifying himself as a poor worker and getting a first year salary of £100,000.

This example also sets limits on the cost of the signal. How much tuition should the business school charge? If the fees for the business school go up above £50,000, even the good worker will choose not to get the degree. In contrast, if the fees drop below £30,000, the poor workers will also get the degree, making the signaling value of the degree disappear. For example, if the government were to announce that because it thinks that education is valuable, it will provide a £20,000 tax credit to anyone who enrolls in a university. Using the numbers in the example above, a degree will cost a good worker £30,000 and a shirker £50,000. Unfortunately, this means both shirkers and good workers will end up getting degrees, destroying the signaling value of the degree. The employer is back in its original situation without any means of distinguishing between good and poor workers and hence will offer £130,000 again. Making education too cheap destroys its value as a signal – even though education may indeed have value in itself as a social good. This may explain why in some countries like India, employers complain that a huge number of engineering students graduate from the country's colleges every year, yet these graduates are essentially unemployable. Since education is heavily subsidized, everyone gets the degree, and hence employers are unable to use it as a signal to distinguish good from poor engineers.

Signals have been discussed everywhere in both biology and economics. Consider for example, why male peacocks have large and colorful tails. It is not enough to say that peahens find large and colorful tails attractive. We have to explain *why* they do. A large colorful tail catches the eye not only of females but also predators such as dogs or leopards. In addition, the weight of the tail makes it difficult for the bird to fly away easily. Hence, a signaling explanation for the existence of peacock tails says that the peacock is essentially signaling that it is bearing a huge handicap. It has survived to adulthood bearing this handicap which means that it is a survivor – and hence would make a great mate. Note that the peahen does not actually have to reason this out. Peahens that mate with peacocks with extra-long tails have more surviving offspring (with larger tails) that go on to procreate more. Eventually, the length of the tail becomes an evolutionary arms race with the number of predators acting as a cap on the maximum length and colorfulness of the tail.

Signaling has even proposed for to explain the existence of strong emotions such as anger, jealousy, and even falling in love. Religions tell us that negative emotions such as anger and jealousy are bad[5] and we need to focus on positive emotions, letting the negative emotions go. Medical books have been written about the negative consequences of anger.[6] So why did we evolve with these emotions? What evolutionary purpose do they serve when they are so toxic to our health? From a signaling perspective, the precise value of the signal is indeed its toxic nature. For example, suppose your children are clamoring to play soccer in the garden with you while you are trying to finish an important memo. Rationally explaining to your children the cost-benefit analysis between playing with them and developing their social skills versus keeping a roof over their heads and eventually being able to send them to college (if you get a promotion thanks to the memo) is unlikely to cut much ice. In fact, few rational arguments will work. In contrast, losing your temper and yelling at them will usually work in getting them out of your hair.

Why does this work? Medical evidence suggests that people increase their risk for a heart attack more than eightfold shortly after an intensely angry episode. Anger can also help bring on strokes and an irregular heartbeat, other research shows. It may lead to sleep problems, excess eating, and insulin resistance, which can help cause diabetes.[7] The ideal would be to *pretend* to get angry which would make the children stop pestering you while simultaneously maintaining an internal zen-like calm. Unfortunately, we are also frighteningly good at detecting when people are faking their emotions, one reason (perhaps) why great actors are paid so much. This is exactly akin to the poor worker pretending to be a good worker – the signal only works when we are not faking anger with the concomitant costs to our health.

Similarly, falling in love with someone can also act as a signal. Here too, the signal is the giving up of control. If I do a careful study of my partner's attractiveness and a cost-benefit analysis of the merits of remaining with her, my partner will know that there is every possibility that I will make the same analysis when a new potential partner comes along. Because she might be dumped easily if a new more attractive partner came along, she would be reluctant to make the commitment to enter into a relationship with me. If I am obviously in love with her, since I cannot control the process, I am also less likely to be able to control the process of falling *out* of love with her, and therefore she might be willing to enter into a relationship with me.

In economics, an example of a signaling model can be seen in the choice of how hard to work in your job. When we begin our jobs, we have two choices to show how hard others perceive us to be working. We can choose a super-hard worker strategy. If we know our boss gets in at 9:00 am, we time our arrival for 8:55 am. If our boss consistently leaves at 6:00 pm, we make sure we leave at 6:05 pm. The other strategy is a super-genius strategy which involves us coming into work late and leaving early, while still finishing the same amount of work as the super-hard worker does. Which is a better strategy to use?

The key is that there are two types of asymmetric information involved here. The first, of course, is signaling how smart you are. Unfortunately, most of the people who are reading this book are unlikely to be manual workers whose output can be clearly measured. So if you adopt a super-genius strategy, your boss is more likely to think that your job is particularly easy rather than you being extremely smart. The consequence of using a super-genius strategy when the boss doesn't understand the difficulty level of the work will mean that you will be given a lot more work.

Yet another example of a signaling model arises when we try to explain why universities grant tenure to university professors.[8] In the U.S. academic system, tenure is a contractual right not to have the position terminated without just cause. More simply, a tenured professor cannot be fired unless she does something illegal. Prima facie, this concept appears untenable in the twenty-first century. With widespread job insecurity even among the highly educated, it appears archaic that a particular group of employees, university faculty, are given life-time employment. In the United States, tenure is sharply binary – a handful of scholars get tenure while a large number of academics get poorly paid untenured posts with little status or security.

Proponents of tenure argue that it preserves the quality of university education, since it gives professors academic freedom to pursue path-breaking research ideas and to freely voice their own opinions without being censured by administrators. Opponents of tenure argue that tenure is part of an outmoded system that encourages professors to pursue research (perhaps of questionable quality) over teaching. Some opponents argue that tenure actually reduces academic freedom because in order to get tenure, academics must conform to the political or academic mainstream.

From an economic point of view, however, tenure can be seen as a simple mechanism for universities to assure themselves of quality research. Recall the two major principal-agent problems – adverse selection and moral hazard. Universities face both these problems: first, they need to hire faculty who will be research-active in the long term – the adverse selection problem. Second, they need to make sure that they offer incentives for the faculty to stay research-active once hired – the moral hazard problem.

Once a professor gains tenure, she cannot be fired. So the tenure process would seem to exacerbate the moral hazard problem. If the university can do nothing to punish the professor, a tenured professor can slack off the rest of her life without fear of being fired. A regular system of performance reviews might appear to be better than tenure here – if a professor starts slacking off, she will be fired on her next review.

However, this system makes the adverse selection process worse – and adverse selection is what will ultimately destroy the university. Consider what it is that makes a university's reputation. Great teachers are memorable to their students, but what really makes a university famous is the quality of its research.

What did professors at the university discover? What did they create? This is what we remember the great universities for. The annual university reputation rankings published by the Times Higher Education group, for example, give twice the weight to research as to teaching. Teaching is measurable. The quality of teachers can be assessed through student evaluations, student signups for elective classes, and so on.

However, basic research by its very nature is unpredictable. Science has become increasingly specialized, so much so, that a scientist in one field will not be able to understand why a discovery in another field has any importance at all. If I show my latest finance research to a sociologist, I confidently expect the sociologist to have a blank expression. This means that the best judges of quality are other professors in the same field.

Now suppose a university were to abolish tenure. Instead, it announces that every five years, there will be a performance review and the ones who have contributed the least to research will be fired (the university will not put that much emphasis on teaching because as noted above, its reputation depends on the ideas that professors generate). Now what is the best strategy for a senior untenured professor in the area? Simple. Interview all the aspiring professors and hire the idiots. In five years, the new untenured professors will all be fired because ex ante they had silly research ideas, and the wise senior professor achieves de facto, though not de jure, tenure. That is the adverse selection problem that the university faces. To solve it, the university says to the senior professor: hire the smart juniors. They will bring fame to the department, bring in more funds from government and industry, and increase the resources available to you. However, your job is safe whatever happens.

Unfortunately, this worsens the moral hazard problem. How do universities solve that problem? They make the tenure process so difficult that only a handful of professors achieve it. In the United States, over 90% of professors do not make tenure in the schools they start in. Why do universities make this hurdle so high? Because universities hope that the handful of professors who do achieve tenure are so driven that they will work hard even though they do not have to. Though, of course, the university acknowledges that this is a hope, not a requirement.

What about signaling in the business world? Consider advertising. You may have seen advertisements that tell you absolutely nothing about the product or the company. Why do companies post such ads? The reason is that firms are not necessarily signaling only to their customers, they are also signaling to their competitors. A firm that buys time to post an ad that has zero customer relevance is like a peacock with a huge tail. It is signaling to its competitors that its cash flows or future prospects are so good that it can burn a million dollars on irrelevant ads and still take on its competitors. It is a warning to competitors not to try to compete.

Screening Models

In some cases, the buyer has more information than the seller. In particular, the buyer knows how desperate he is to buy. For example, a travel agent does not know how pressed for time a customer might be. A health insurance firm does not know whether its potential customer is healthy or dying but would prefer the former. A car insurance firm does not know whether customers are good or bad drivers. In each case, the seller has an incentive to elicit this information from the buyer. This is the essence of screening models, where the less informed party offers a selection of choices. The choice picked by the more informed party reveals his type to the less informed party.

Let's take an example to nail this down. Suppose an airline is offering a luxury vacation package to Africa on a particular weekend with air transportation from your city. What do you know, as the buyer, that the airline does not? You know just how pressed for time you are. If you are a business executive, for example, you may have a limited number of weekends to take a holiday in a year, and you have to go only on these weekends. In contrast, if you were a tenured[9] professor, you could go whenever you wanted.

How would the airline figure out your type? The agent couldn't ask you whether you were pressed for time because you would say of course not, you were not pressed for time. Therefore, the airline screens on convenience. Flights in the middle of the day are much more likely to be taken by business executives and hence are much more expensive. Really early morning flights or overnight red-eye flights are more likely to be taken by tourists and hence are likely to be cheaper. A flight that involves a Saturday night stay over is likely to be cheaper. Why? Who is more likely to stay over on a Saturday night? A business executive is in a strange city by herself and would like to get home to her family. Since the ticket is paid for by her company, she is indifferent to the price. In contrast, tourists are happy to be getting an extra day to stay over at a cheaper price.

Another screening device used by airlines is comfort. Economy class seats are singularly uncomfortable compared to business class seats. Is it not possible for an airline to design more comfortable economy class seats? Of course it is. But the airline knows that if it uses more comfortable economy class seats, some business executives may say that the seat is comfortable enough for them to stay in economy rather than upgrading to business.

Similarly, on many flights, business class passengers board first. Economy class passengers remain waiting in line for the business class passengers to put their carryon luggage in overhead compartments and settle down before they can board. Since the business class passengers are in the front of the plane, it makes more sense for the economy class passengers to board before the business class passengers. However, the discomfort suffered by economy class passengers is precisely the point. Some of them may look at the business class passengers and say, "If only I had upgraded, I'd be settling down and sneering at the economy passengers instead of waiting impatiently in line."

Another example of companies that use screening models are private health insurers. These insurers make money by enrolling healthy patients while minimizing the probability that they have to treat sick patients. The greater the proportion of sick patients in the population, the lower the profit margin becomes. So how do they distinguish healthy from sick patients? They may choose to require health tests for all the people applying for insurance. This is likely to be expensive, though, because they would have to pay the doctors to administer the tests. In the old days, before the Internet, some insurance companies were located at the top of very tall buildings without elevators. If you were healthy enough to climb the stairs to get to the insurance company, you would be given your insurance.

Another cheap way out is to exclude pre-existing conditions. This exclusion criterion eliminates patients who choose to apply for insurance only because they are ill. Several governments have proposed eliminating the use of pre-existing conditions to deny coverage, including the United States. If insurance companies are not allowed to use pre-existing conditions, the only way to get cheap coverage is to mandate compulsory insurance for everyone in the population, regardless of their being sick or healthy. This way, the healthy people subsidize the sick people.

A third example of firms that use screening models are car insurance firms. What kind of drivers do car insurance firms want? Obviously, they want safe drivers. In countries like the UK, insurance companies maintain a register of claims. You get a no-claims bonus if you have driven for several years without making a claim. However, if you have an accident, your no-claims bonus is automatically reduced, and your insurance price goes up.

Suppose you have just obtained a driving license, though. This means that you have no driving history and no no-claims bonus. How does the insurance company figure out what type of driver you are? One way would be to check the size of your deductible. If you choose a high deductible, that means you are committing to pay the first portion of any claim from your own pocket. The high deductible implies that this portion is large. Hence, the insurance company knows that you believe yourself to be a safe driver and so it can offer you a low rate. In contrast, if you choose a low deductible, it means you think that you are very likely to have an accident and the insurance company will therefore charge you a very high rate.

Banking is another area where signaling and screening models are important but not necessarily in the way you may think. What would be a good screening mechanism for a bank to determine who is a good borrower? An obvious answer might be the level of interest rates. Is this really a good screen? Suppose the bank were to raise interest rates, from 5% to 25%.

Who would be willing to pay the higher rates? In the presence of limited liability, the only borrowers who would be willing to agree to a rate of 25% or higher would be the ones with no intention of paying the loan back. They would agree to the loan, take the money, and then declare bankruptcy.

In the presence of extreme asymmetric information therefore, banks are more likely to ration credit than raise interest rates. This may be one reason why, after the 2008 financial crisis, even though bank borrowing rates were extremely low, banks were making no efforts to lend. The asymmetric information generated in the credit crisis was so large that banks could not distinguish good borrowers from bad borrowers. Even though government bond rates were almost zero, banks were unsure that their own loans would ever be paid back.

Another way for bankers to determine who is likely to be a good borrower is to monitor them more closely. However, monitoring costs money. It is therefore easier to borrow $5 million from a bank than it is to borrow $50. The fixed monitoring costs are the same whether the bank lends $5 million or $50. Interestingly, micro finance companies manage to make profits on loans that are less than $50. How do they do this?

One of the pioneers of this type of process is Grameen Bank, a bank that successfully lends in Bangladesh. The average loan size is tiny. How does Grameen find out who is a good borrower if it cannot afford to monitor each borrower? The answer is that Grameen lends to a community of villagers, not just one individual villager. Basically, it understands that the people who are best positioned to monitor any individual villager are her neighbors. So in lending to a group of villagers, Grameen tells each of them that if anyone in the group defaults, the entire group of borrowers will be cut off. Hence, all of the individual villagers have incentives to monitor their neighbors to ensure that their neighbors are not squandering their loan amounts.

Corporate Governance

These ideas of asymmetric information and pooling and separating equilibriums feed directly into the theme that started the book. In Chapter 2, we considered in whose interests should the firm be managed (stakeholders and shareholders), and we concluded that the firm should be managed in the interests of the shareholders. This was because they were paid after everyone else in the firm had been paid off and because they were not protected much by explicit contracts. Hence, they would be most nervous about giving their money to managers of firms.

But why do we need shareholders at all? Can't the manager manage and run her own firm? If she could, this would be just like the situation of the self-sufficient farmer running his own farm. With no asymmetric information problems, there would be no corporate governance problems. Unfortunately, the manager usually does not have either enough capital of her own to invest or else she wants to cash out her holdings. Therefore she needs external capital, and she raises this from shareholders. The problem is that the manager is the expert, not the shareholders. The shareholders have less information and expertise than the manager. They need the manager's expertise to generate returns on the funds they have entrusted to the manager. This is a separation of brains and capital.

Will competition not take care of corporate governance? For example, firms are competing in the marketplace all the time. This forces them to minimize costs. These costs include the costs of raising capital. So every time the firm makes an investment decision, it will ask the external market for money. Good corporate governance allows firms to show investors that their managers will not simply steal their money. Because the firms are competing to raise money, they will also compete on corporate governance, and only the best governed firms will survive.

This mechanism works only if firms go to the market every single time they have to make an investment decision. Unfortunately, they do not. Firms do not necessarily synchronize their financing decisions with their investment decisions. Production capital is highly specific, and if shareholders give their money to firms, they don't see anything back for several years.

So why do shareholders not write explicit contracts (like the other stakeholders do) protecting them in case anything untoward happens? The problem is that writing such a contract is almost impossible since most future contingencies cannot be anticipated, let alone written into an explicit contract.

For example, suppose you are a shareholder in an umbrella company. If the weather is bad in Cambridge this year, the manager promises to pay you a 20% return; otherwise, the return is 2%. What is bad weather, though? Let us be more specific. If it rains more than 300 days a year, the manager promises to pay you a 20% return, otherwise 2%. But wait, how much rain is rain? What about a drizzle? A dampness in the air? Suppose it rains for only 10 minutes? But it's a deluge? The end result is that even if the manager is motivated to write a complete explicit contract, she cannot. Most future contingencies are hard to describe and predict, and as a result, complete contracts are infeasible.[10]

Hence, the question becomes who makes the decision when something happens that is not in the explicit contract? One possibility is that the shareholders ask for these rights before handing over their money. They give money to the manager on the condition that they retain all the residual control rights. Any time something unexpected happens, the shareholders get to decide what to do. However, this does not work, because the shareholders are not qualified or informed enough to decide what to do – that was the very reason why they hired the manager in the first place. As a result, the manager ends up with substantial residual control rights and discretion to allocate funds as she chooses.

What will shareholders be nervous about? What are the ways in which managers can steal shareholder funds? The easiest way is outright theft. Economists call this *expropriation* and have documented a number of ways in which expropriation happens. For example, managers can set up their own private companies to which they sell the output of their firms at low or zero prices. They will then go on to sell this output at market prices and put the proceeds into their own pockets. Similarly, they can sell inputs to the publicly traded employing firms at very high prices.

Alternatively, managers can try to meet their own goals and instead of working on the behalf of shareholders. They can try to maximize firm size instead of maximizing shareholder value, because a large firm is more difficult to be taken over than a small firm. Managers can promote favored subordinates, their own family members, or their friends to high-ranking positions and this is also easier to do in a large firm.

A third way in which managers can steal shareholder funds is the consumption of perquisites. The use of corporate jets, the installation of plush carpets in offices, or golf club memberships are possible ways in which managers can consume unnecessary perks. Of course, managers will claim that these are neither unnecessary nor perks. For example, a golf club membership can be justified on the grounds that this helps the manager to identify new business opportunities through his golfing networks. The use of a corporate jet can be justified on the basis that it saves the manager time in going to the airport, checking in for security, sleeping in an uncomfortable seat, and then eventually arriving too tired to make a good business deal. Again, shareholders, not being experts, cannot determine if the manager is telling the truth and this is really necessary for the company, or if the manager is lying and just consuming perks.

Because of all these reasons, shareholders, unable to enter into explicit contracts and unable to enforce implicit contracts, are very reluctant to trust managers with their money, unless the manager can commit to not stealing it. Corporate governance mechanisms act either as signals or screens to show shareholders that their money is safe. What mechanisms are these? In the rest of this chapter, I will briefly discuss four major types.

The first type of mechanism is an incentive contract. An inocntive contract is a contingent long-term contract that ex ante aligns managerial interests with those of shareholders. This means that the contract pays off only if the manager maximizes shareholder value and does not pay off if the manager destroys shareholder value. Examples of such contracts are stock options, share ownership, or the threat of dismissal if the share price is low. If the manager chooses not to work hard on behalf of the shareholders (the reasoning goes), the share price will not rise, and hence the options will cease to have any value. In order for the manager to be paid, he therefore has to work in the interests of shareholders. This solves the moral hazard problem. Unfortunately, some researchers have argued that it does not solve the adverse selection problem. In other words, what kind of manager is attracted by a large stock option payment? Presumably the kind of manager who believes that he can in fact drive up the price of the shares substantially. This manager is likely to be confident and perhaps even overconfident about his own abilities. These researchers have shown that there is a negative relationship between the amount of money paid in the form of options and the long-term performance of the firm.

The second type of mechanism involves legal constraints. Legal constraints differ across countries, and the nature of these legal obligations determines how willing shareholders are to invest the money in the firm. For example, many countries give shareholders the right to vote on important matters such as mergers and liquidations, as well as to elect the board of directors. However, voting rights tend to be expensive to exercise and to enforce. In some countries, shareholders cannot vote by post. They actually have to show up at shareholder meetings in order to vote. In many cases, firms hold their annual general meetings in remote and exotic locations precisely because they would like to make it more difficult for shareholders to get there.

Even if shareholders can vote, the value of their votes differs across countries. For example, even though shareholders may have the right to elect a board of directors, the board need not necessarily represent shareholder interests. In particular, it is important to remember who chooses the directors. In many cases, management proposes the directors. Sometimes, the chairman of the board is also the CEO of the firm. These are all corporate governance issues that have been extensively studied across the world and across time periods. What should be the optimal size of the board? What should the proportion of inside to outside directors be? In countries like India and China, the government has mandated a proportion of independent outside directors on the board. But where do these directors come from? In a country such as India, the pool of independent directors is not very deep. So to meet their mandate, a number of firms ended up hiring the same qualified directors. Unfortunately, these busy directors, even if they do not have conflicts of interest, may not have the time to monitor the firms appropriately. Finally, boards are rather blunt instruments. The evidence across the world indicates that boards are typically quite passive except in extreme circumstances. A major performance disaster is usually required before the board actually acts.

The third mechanism is a concentration of ownership. When cash flow rights are concentrated in the hands of a small number of investors, these investors have incentives to monitor the managers. Moreover, these large shareholders find it easier to coordinate among themselves than when the control rights are split among many small shareholders. Essentially, concentration of ownership increases legal protection. Concentration of ownership varies across the world. In smaller German companies, for example, the norm is family controlled majority ownership or pyramids. Pyramids enable the ultimate owners to control the firm's assets with the least amount of capital necessary. In the United States and the UK, pyramidal shareholdings are relatively uncommon. There are legal restrictions on large ownership stakes and the exercise of control by banks or mutual funds. Both the United States and the UK fought anti-pyramidal campaigns, changing closely-held shareholder structures to the current widely dispersed shareholder base found in these countries. Concentration of ownership, especially family ownership, allows shareholders to control managers, but it creates new types of agency problems. For example, it is now possible for the majority shareholders to expropriate wealth from the minority shareholders in the firm.

The fourth mechanism is the hostile takeover market. In the United States, large outside shareholders are not very common. So you need a different mechanism to make sure that managers are working on behalf of shareholders. This is a hostile takeover. Takeover targets are often poorly performing firms, and the target managers are removed once a takeover succeeds. Unfortunately, takeovers are sufficiently expensive that only major performance failures are likely to be addressed. Politically, they are also vulnerable because they are opposed by managerial lobbies. Finally, takeovers can actually increase agency costs when the bidding firm management overpays for targets that bring them private benefits of control.

At the end of the day, every corporate governance mechanism has its own problems. There are no codes of best practice for corporate governance. While many governments and agencies publish such codes, these are largely box-ticking exercises. Going back to our earlier principles of screening and signaling models, if adhering to a code is mandatory, it ceases to be a signal. In other words, if a good firm would like to distinguish itself from a poor firm, it has to go beyond the code to find a signal that the market believes is efficiently strong to distinguish it from a poorly managed firm. This, however, is the firm's responsibility, not the market's. If the firm does not manage to convince the market that it is a good firm, it will raise less capital at less attractive terms, than if it is able to do so.

Notes

1. If we think about these issues at all.
2. Nitpicking readers might object at this point, that if no plums are sold at all, how does the buyer know that 70% of the cars in the market are lemons while 30% are plums? To get around this minor problem, we assume that a mandatory testing agency checks every car for vehicle safety, roadworthiness, and exhaust emissions every year. The mandatory part is necessary to avoid what are called selection problems. In the UK, this is called the annual MOT (Ministry of Transport) test, and results from the MOT test are assumed to be public information. A really nitpicking reader might follow up by asking why owners will not have to have their cars repaired after an MOT test failure. In this case, you can argue that the owner knows that the car will fail the MOT test and will seek to sell it before the test. A really, really nitpicking reader might argue that in that case, the statistics should correspond to the last test, which may not have any bearing on the current statistical probability of getting a lemon. In this case, you can think up more ingenious arguments as to why this is not the case, making the note even longer. Or give your heckler a black eye.
3. Economists don't do that obviously. Most of us avoid physical confrontation. So we just raise an eyebrow and say superciliously that the answer is obvious to anyone with brains (except if the questioner is larger than us). Or if it is a student and we are feeling mean and nasty, we assign it as a homework problem for the class.
4. I leave it to the reader to decide if the psychopath description refers to a willingness to kill or in a willingness to do this on a government salary.
5. They don't really say much about falling in love (as opposed to loving someone).
6. See, for example, Redford Williams, *Anger Kills: Seventeen Strategies for Controlling the Hostility That Can Harm Your Health* (New York: Harper Torch, 1998).
7. See, for example, Jean Whalen, "Angry Outbursts Really Do Hurt Your Health, Doctors Find," *Wall Street Journal*, March 23, 2015.

8. Raghavendra Rau, "The Economic Rationale for Tenured Professors, *Financial Times*, June 1, 2014.
9. Or more precisely a retired professor, since tenured professors never stop working, obviously.
10. How is it that bondholders can (and do) write explicit contracts? That is because bondholders have much smaller asymmetric information problems than shareholders. They are not concerned with the future growth prospects of the company – all they care about is being paid back. The formal financial statements of the firm give them a lot of contracting information that they can use to write formal explicit contracts laying out the rights they have if the firm does not pay them back. Shareholders, in contrast, are depending a lot on future growth prospects of the firm – a much more ill-defined concept that is difficult to explicitly contract on.

7 Market Efficiency

Learning Points

■ Why is market efficiency so important?
■ What does it mean for a market to be efficient?
■ The types of market efficiency
■ Testing market efficiency
■ Evidence inconsistent with market efficiency
■ Systematic investor biases
■ Limits to arbitrage

The last major idea in this book also focuses on information. In Chapter 6, we allowed for the possibility that the buyer and seller of any asset may have different information regarding its true value. Here we examine if investors process the information they receive in different ways, so that the market price does not correctly reflect the fundamental value of the asset.

Why Is Market Efficiency So Important?

Let us start by thinking how we set prices. Suppose we want to buy an airline ticket online. What do we do? Most of us would start by using an online search engine to find prices. But do we buy the airline ticket right away? Many of us would not. We would go back the next day and search for the same ticket again. If the ticket price has gone up, we would be a little more eager to buy. We might be willing to wait an additional day, but if prices go up again on the second day, we would be much more likely to buy immediately. In contrast, if the ticket price has gone down, we would be much more willing to wait. If the ticket goes down in price yet again on the second day, we will be willing to wait even longer.

In essence, what we are doing is estimating supply and demand. Rising ticket prices signal to us that there is high demand and low supply. Falling ticket prices signal the opposite. Companies use much the same information to make investment decisions. If prices are rising on particular types of goods, they will try to manufacture more. What all this means is that prices give us very useful information about supply and demand, expected economic growth, discount rates, volatility, and a whole host of other macroeconomic factors. Incorrect prices compromise both business and household planning.

Similarly, prices also matter for corporate governance. For example, if we were to buy shares in a firm, and the share price goes up from the time we bought the shares, we are likely to conclude that the firm managers are good. If the share price has dropped precipitously since the time we purchased the shares, we are much more likely to conclude that our managers are idiots. Again, incorrect prices compromise this role.

What Does It Mean for a Market to Be Efficient?

So how did the efficient market hypothesis (EMH) develop? Until the 1960s, there were two basic approaches to investing. The first was called technical analysis, and the second was called fundamental analysis. Technical analysis, also called charting, assumes that we can find good investments simply by examining past price or return patterns. We do not need to know anything about a company, including its name, its products, its governance, sales, assets, or anything else. All we need to know is the way the company shares have traded over the past year or two. Technical analysis has assumed new and ostensibly more sophisticated forms since the 1960s. Today, for example, it is called algorithmic trading or day trading, but the basic ideas remain the same.

In contrast, fundamental analysis assumes that good investments can be found through a careful analysis of financial and economic data. Under this approach, we need to find out everything possible about the company in order to find out the value of its securities. This approach, which is as venerable as technical analysis, forms the basis of valuation by many analysts and investment companies such as Berkshire Hathaway. In fact, one of the pioneering textbooks in this area is Graham and Dodd's *Security Analysis* which was written in 1934 and is still in print today.

So what happened in the 1960s? Economics made huge advancements, in particular, in an area called general equilibrium theory. Finance became a respectable academic field. General equilibrium models were easy to derive when we assume competition and when security markets seem to best approximate the theoretical model of perfect competition. The emerging intuition was that if the market is perfectly competitive, there is no such thing as a free lunch.

This led naturally to the definition of an efficient capital market: An efficient capital market is a market that is efficient in processing *information*. The prices of securities observed at any time are based on "correct" evaluations of all information available at that time. In other words, in an efficient market, prices fully reflect all available information.

This research effort that gave rise to this definition, proposed by Gene Fama in 1970, was partly instrumental in winning him the Nobel Prize over forty years later. Of course, not everybody believes this. For example, Warren Buffett, chairman, CEO, and largest shareholder of Berkshire Hathaway, is reported to have said, "I would be a bum in the street with a tin cup if markets were always efficient." Similarly, Larry Summers, former U.S. treasury secretary and former president of Harvard University, colorfully dismissed the EMH, beginning an unpublished paper with the phrase "There are idiots. Look around."

But the definition of market efficiency is more subtle than it appears at first glance. Let us take an example. Suppose the Mighty Oak company is developing a new computer that would be twice as powerful as computers currently available on the market. This is the only project the company has, and the new computer is currently scheduled to be brought to market two years from today. The net present value of the project is $100 million, and so the company has to be worth at least $100 million. Let us suppose that today, October 1, the company announces that a well-known professor will join the workforce on January 1 next year to help develop the new computer. The professor will significantly improve the chance that the computer will be brought to market early. How much earlier? Let us say one year, so with the professor, the new computer will be brought to market one year from today. Using option theory from Chapter 4, we figure out the value of this early-to-market option is worth $10 million to the company.

Is this good or bad news for the company? Prima facie, it appears to be good news. But we do not really know this until we figure out what the professor will be paid. If, for example, the professor is actually paid $20 million for improving the value of the company by $10 million, the professor is destroying shareholder value to the tune of $10 million. To simplify matters, let us assume that the professor is paid $1 million for his services. Subtracting this from the value of the improvement in the project value leaves us with the conclusion that hiring hiding the professor would make the firm better off by $9 million. We are still not done unfortunately. The question we are concerned about is *when* the market incorporates this good news.

There are three possible dates: first, the date of the original announcement, October 1. Here the professor has not joined the company yet, and no new computer has been developed. Second, January 1 next year. Here the professor has just joined the firm, but no new computer has been developed yet. Third, October 1 next year. Here the professor has been with the firm for one year, and the new computer has been developed.

The obvious answer is October 1 next year. That would mean that on October 1 next year, the value of the firm would go up by $9 million. However, one of the key assumptions of market efficiency is competition, and lots of it. What would happen on September 30 next year? A competitive trader, knowing that the price will go up by $9 million on October 1, will be trying to buy shares ahead of everybody else on September 30. An even more competitive trader will try to buy on September 29. Iterating this process backwards leads to the inevitable conclusion that hypercompetitive traders, trying to stay one step ahead of anyone else, will all try to buy the shares today, when the professor has not yet joined the company and the new computer has not been developed. Since everybody is trying to buy the shares today, the value of the company will jump *today* by $9 million. What this example illustrates is that prices react to information, not to events.

And an implication of market efficiency is that in a brutally competitive efficient market, it is impossible to consistently make abnormal returns on the basis of information. More precisely, because of the brutal competition, if you want to make money on the stock market, you have to be first in line to trade the misvalued shares *every* time. And there is no way to guarantee this if everyone is jostling for first place in the line.

What is the economics behind the EMH? An unsurprising answer is that the market price P is the outcome of supply and demand. The EMH can be thought of as a hypothesis about the relative shape/position of the supply and demand curves. What is the supply curve for any security? Securities are supplied by the firm, so what we are trying to do is to plot how the firm changes the amount of securities it has on offer when prices change. Supply is set by firms on the primary market, either by issuing more shares or buying back shares. How do firms react to short-term price fluctuations? Typically, they don't. So the supply curve is essentially a vertical line in the short term. This is illustrated in Figure 7.1. Firms do not change the amount of shares they issue when prices change on a daily basis. Economists say that the supply of shares is price-inelastic in the short run.

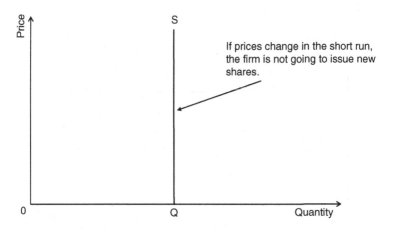

Figure 7.1 The supply curve for shares

Daily price movements in the shares are driven by fluctuations in aggregate demand, the quantity demanded by investors in total, as a function of the price P. If we assume no new information coming to the market, then a share is like any normal good. As the price goes up, the quantity demanded goes down. This is illustrated in Figure 7.2.

The aggregate demand curve is the horizontal sum of all investors' personal demand curves, as illustrated in Figure 7.3. When prices are high relative to investor expectations, the quantity demanded is low, but as more and more investors enter

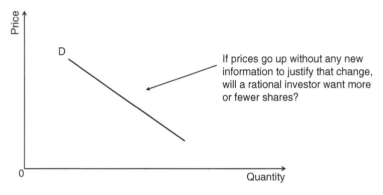

If prices go up without any new information to justify that change, will a rational investor want more or fewer shares?

Figure 7.2 The individual demand curve for shares

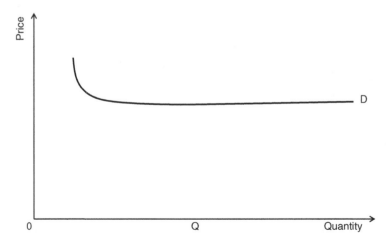

Figure 7.3 The aggregate demand curve for shares

the market, the demand curve smoothes out as each individual investor becomes relatively unimportant relative to the mass. Hence, any individual investor demand becomes insignificant compared to the large mass of investors.

Now combining the aggregate demand curves and the supply curve, Figure 7.4 shows that the price is set at the point where the firm's supply curve intersects the aggregate demand curve.

The EMH hypothesis says that the supply curve intersects the aggregate demand curve precisely when the aggregate demand curve is flat. This simple statement conceals a lot of information. For example, the aggregate demand curve is not likely to be flat when there is little demand (there are few investors, so small changes in demand will change prices a lot). In these cases, the EMH will not necessarily hold, since individual investor beliefs can change the price and quantity demanded. At the EMH point, individual investors are insignificant relative to the mass of investors, so no individual investor can change the price by buying and selling. This implies that the EMH is more likely to hold in liquid markets with lots of investors than in small illiquid markets.

At this point where the supply curve intersects the aggregate demand curve, the EMH asserts that if the aggregate demand curve is flat, the market price P is given by the security's

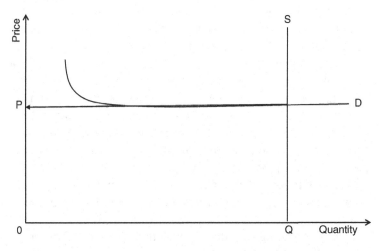

Figure 7.4 The aggregate demand curve and supply curve for shares

fundamental value, E[P*]. The fundamental value of the security is given by an NPV analysis in Chapter 2 as:

$$E[P^*] \equiv \sum_{t=1}^{\infty} \frac{E[CF_t]}{(1+E[R])^t} \tag{7.1}$$

Here E[R] is the rational discount rate, while E[CF] is the expected cash flows.

Under what conditions might the supply curve intersect the aggregate demand curve precisely at the point when the aggregate demand curve is flat?

There are three possible scenarios. First, suppose, all investors rationally use equation 7.1 to derive the fundamental value of any security. Specifically, they value securities on the basis of their expected discounted cash flows and accurately use all info to determine E[P*]. If the market price of the security drops even a fraction below E[P*], say even a penny below, *every* rational investor demands a lot more. Similarly, every rational investor will demand a lot less (even short-selling if necessary) if P > E[P*]. This will make the aggregate demand curve flat at P = E[P*].

Second, even if some investors are irrational in that they do not use equation 7.1 to value securities, their uncorrelated misperceptions cancel out. For example, if optimists think that P < E[P*] and an equal number of pessimists think P > E[P*], they can trade with each other without affecting P. So in equilibrium, assuming P = E[P*] to start with, P = E[P*] remains true.

Third, suppose there is a huge mass of unbalanced investors who all simultaneously believe that a security is overpriced (P > E[P*]) and are all panicking, trying to sell shares. Even in this case, markets will stay efficient as long as arbitrage[1] is unlimited. Arbitrageurs are big rational investors who do use equation 7.1, rationally compute E[P*], and trade big quantities when P ≠ E[P*]. So even though everyone else may be panicking, these rational arbitrageurs will step in, buying large quantities of shares and driving prices back to fundamental values.

How do arbitrageurs do this without taking risk? They typically form arbitrage portfolios that include the mispriced security and an opposite position in a perfect cash flow substitute. The idea is to exploit mispricing while hedging cash flow risk. For example, suppose you notice that a handbag is sold more cheaply in a foreign country than your own. You might consider buying a whole host of those bags, bringing them back to your home country, and selling them for a markup. Is this arbitrage? Not necessarily, since there are risks. Suppose you buy the bags, but between the time you paid for the bags in the foreign currency and the time you sell the bags, your home currency drops in value. This exchange rate risk reduces the value of the arbitrage opportunity. Similarly, you need to account for the cost of your plane ticket, the price of the excess baggage, or the risk that you will be stopped by customs and questioned as to why you are buying so many handbags. All these risks make an apparently obvious arbitrage opportunity not quite so risk-free in practice.

The upshot is that markets will be efficient as long as everyone is rationally using formulae like equation 7.1 (and the others in the book) to derive prices and make trading decisions, *or* as long as investors do not have correlated misperceptions (different investors treat new information differently; they do not systematically agree that it is good or bad news), *or* even if they have correlated misperceptions, unconstrained arbitrage is possible.

As long as these three conditions are fulfilled, the EMH says that it is impossible to consistently make abnormal returns on the basis of information. Now, this is a very dismal view of the world. And obviously no one (except perhaps finance professors) believes wholeheartedly in market efficiency; otherwise, there would not be hundreds of Wall Street traders out there, all trying to make money. Why doesn't everyone believe in the theory of market efficiency? One possibility is that the truth is less interesting. For example, suppose you make money on the stock market today. Your envious friends ask you how you did that. You can say, well, you know markets are efficient – sometimes you make money, sometimes you lose money. This time I made money, but there are lots of times I lost money. That kind of sounds a little boring, doesn't it? Alternatively, you can say, well, I did a lot of careful analysis of the way the market was moving, the way the CEO behaved on his last conference call, the questions the analysts were asking, and I thought that something was wrong, so I shorted the shares. That sounds a lot more intelligent and interesting. In addition, there are optical illusions, mirages, and apparent patterns in charts of market returns. Human beings are amazing pattern detectors. We can detect patterns in anything, as evidenced by our beliefs in astrology. It is very tough for human beings to believe that market movements can essentially be random, especially when we can *see* that information moves prices.

It gets even tougher when we read about traders who have made lots of money trading on the stock market. Examples include George Soros, who was called the man who broke the Bank of England, partly because he took an opposing stance to the Bank of England in 1992 and prevailed, helping to drive the UK out of the European exchange rate mechanism; John Paulson, who runs the hedge fund Paulson & Company, earning $3.7 billion in 2007 by shorting the U.S. housing market; and Warren Buffett, the legendary chairman and CEO of Berkshire Hathaway, who has earned extraordinary returns over the past fifty years. How is it possible for us to say that it is impossible to consistently make abnormal returns on the basis of information if Warren Buffett can earn extraordinary returns over a period of fifty years?

Let us go back to that definition. There are three terms we need to highlight in the definition: It is impossible to *consistently* make *abnormal* returns on the basis of *information*.

First, let us take the term *consistently*. Market efficiency is not saying that it is not possible to make abnormal returns. There will be occasions when you can make abnormal returns. The key is not to bet your day job on consistently earning abnormal returns.[2]

Second, what does the term *abnormal* mean? Since *abnormal* means *not* normal, we need first to define what normal returns are.

Testing Market Efficiency

The problem with equation 7.1 is that the EMH does *not* say anything about which E[R] or E[CF] to use. It just says that what the market uses is "right." In other words, the EMH asserts that P equals the best possible estimate of P* that can be made using a given "information set." So how can we test the EMH? The direct approach would be to compute E[P*] and see if it equals P. But there are two problems: How do we forecast the cash flows, CF? And what is the right discount rate, E[R]? These are both hard problems. So in an indirect approach, what we actually do is test whether, using a given information set, we can forecast "abnormal" returns (i.e., returns over and above the normal E[R]). This avoids having to forecast the cash flows, but we still need to take a position on the benchmark E[R].

Drawing on Chapter 3, we know that one obvious candidate is the capital asset pricing model (CAPM) in equation 3.8. The CAPM has been extensively tested since its initial derivation. Sadly, those tests have shown that the explanatory power of the CAPM in explaining returns is relatively low. So a number of alternative asset pricing models have been derived including the Fama-French (FF) three-factor model, the FF five-factor model, the consumption CAPM (the CCAPM), and the arbitrage pricing theory (APT). Unfortunately, none of them does a perfect job in explaining returns. Each model makes debatable assumptions, and each has its own implementation problems.

What this means for us is that every test of market efficiency involves two hypotheses, the first that we are using the right asset pricing model (the same one investors are using), and the second, given that we are using the right model, we cannot make abnormal returns.

This is called the joint hypothesis problem and is a subtle but very important problem. For example, suppose I were to tell you that my asset pricing model predicts that the normal return on the stock exchange index is 10% per year. You make 15%. There are three possibilities to explain your performance:

1. The model is correct, and the market is inefficient (in that you are making abnormal returns).

2. The model is incorrect, but the market is efficient: Perhaps the expected market return is indeed 15%, and you are not earning abnormal returns.
3. The model is incorrect, *and* the market is inefficient: Perhaps the expected market return is 12%, and you are earning abnormal returns, just not the ones predicted by the model.

Unfortunately given our lack of knowledge on precisely what risk is, we have no way of distinguishing these three possibilities. The simple fact that a or and mutual fund manager claims to earn abnormal returns beating a benchmark that she specifies does not mean that the market is inefficient and that she is taking advantage of this inefficiency. It could just mean that she is using an inappropriate benchmark.[3]

The Types of Market Efficiency

Third, what does the term *information* mean? We can think about three sets of information that might be used to form our expectations of fundamental value E[P*]:

1. Past prices/returns
2. All publicly available information
3. All public and private information

Each of these leads to three (progressively stronger) notions of market efficiency:

1. Weak form: all information in past prices is efficiently included.
2. Semi-strong-form: all public information is efficiently included.
3. Strong-form: all information is efficiently included, whether public or private.

A weak-form efficient market incorporates all information in past prices. We don't need any information about the firm itself apart from its returns or prices. Consider a simple rule: "If volume in a particular stock hits a certain minimum threshold and the 50-day moving average of the stock's price crosses above the 200-day moving average, buy $100 worth of shares. If volumes hit the threshold and the 50-day moving average crosses below the 200-day moving average, sell $100 of shares." The idea behind this rule is that there is high demand (volume has crossed a high threshold) and the short-term price (50-day moving average) is higher than its long-term average (200-day moving average), the share is likely to go up in value, so it is a good idea to buy these shares. Rules like this are the essence of technical analysis or algorithmic trading. The weak-form EMH says that rules like this don't work. To put it another way, day trading might be fun but won't consistently earn you enough money to quit your day job.

Weak-form EMH has been tested extensively. Researchers have tried to find if today's returns can be used to predict tomorrow's returns, this week's returns can be used to predict next week's returns, or similarly for other periods. The short answer: They can't. After controlling for the benchmark returns, past prices appear to have almost no explanatory power for future returns. This is not entirely surprising. If there were obvious patterns (low prices today imply low prices tomorrow, for example), they would instantly be arbitraged away. The researchers tried very elaborate trading rules, not just simple trends. The uniform conclusion from these tests is that even if abnormal returns could be forecast (slightly) using past prices, trading costs would probably eat up any profits.

A semi-strong efficient market incorporates all public information about a company into its prices. As an example, while we may have seen the movie, *Titanic,* depicting the sinking of the ship on April 15, 1912, most non-economists probably did not notice that the director, James Cameron, left out the vitally interesting news[4] that the ship's owner, the International Mercantile Marine Company, spent $7.5 million to build the ship but only had had insurance for $5.5 million. Within two days, the market capitalization of IMM dropped by $2.5 million. In an era without email, helicopter news cameras, or Twitter, the market took less than two days to react to this information. $2 million was the difference in insurance value and the extra $0.5 million was perhaps due to expected lower cash flows due to lost reputation. The easiest way to understand how market efficiency works is to visualize returns using an event study graph in Figure 7.5.

The only reaction possible if the market is semi-strong efficient is the immediate reaction on the day the information becomes publicly available, the announcement day. It should be impossible to consistently earn abnormal returns by buying on the announcement day because all hypercompetitive traders are buying on that day driving the price up instantaneously. In contrast, suppose you aggregate 1,000 events of the same type, say all mergers, and find that the price takes time to react to information. It goes up slowly on good news – it under-reacts. Then you don't have to be hypercompetitive. You can take your time buying and still guarantee that you can make money. Similarly, suppose you find that the market consistently over-reacts and then corrects itself. In this case, you just short-sell the shares on the announcement day and make money when the prices subsequently decline. Semi-strong EMH says that both these alternative strategies are effectively useless. To put it another way, fundamental analysis is worthless.

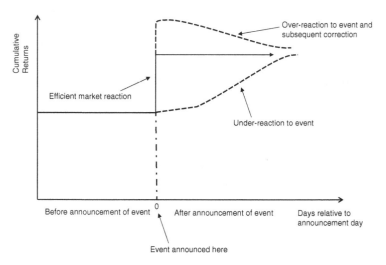

Figure 7.5 Event study: Reactions of stock prices to new information in efficient markets

Another way to examine semi-strong market efficiency is to study the performance of mutual fund and hedge fund managers. These managers claim that they are specialists who are continually in the market researching investment opportunities. Surely, their returns are better than those of non-specialist retail investors who have other things to do with their lives? Researchers have examined the performance of mutual fund and hedge fund managers in general for the past sixty-five years. They have used alternative benchmarking models, alternative approaches to measuring performance, and ways of controlling for statistical biases. Very little evidence has emerged that mutual fund managers are indeed skilled – that they consistently earn arbitrage returns above appropriate risk-adjusted benchmarks. This growing realization has led to the growth of passive fund companies such as Vanguard that focus on buying the entire market. In other words, they implicitly assume that markets are efficient in that no investor is able to consistently beat the market. Hence, a passive fund offers a cheap way of diversifying but does not expect to beat the market.

How then do we explain the great investors? Warren Buffett, for example, is open about using fundamental analysis to identifying undervalued firms. How has he been able to earn excess returns for over fifty years? If you invested $100 in Berkshire shares in 1965, at the end of 2014, you would have had $1,826,163. An investment in the S&P500 would have given you $11,196.[5] We need to note that all the great investors are identified on an ex post basis. In other words, what is important for us is not whether Warren Buffett has earned extraordinary returns for the past half-century but whether we can identify the next Warren Buffett. Absent a time machine, there is absolutely no value from showing that Warren Buffett was an extraordinary investor.

But isn't it interesting that some fund managers have had phenomenal records? Doesn't the existence of these managers show that it must be possible to beat the market and that there is hope for the rest of us? Alas no. Meet the coin toss game.

Let's line up all the investors in the world and ask them all to toss one coin each. Including all countries around the world, let us suppose that there are ½ billion investors.[6] If the coin comes up heads, we tell them that they have beaten the market and that they may continue to play on. If they come up tails, they leave. After the first coin toss, there are approximately ¼ billion investors who have beaten the market by sheer luck. After the second, there are 125 million investors who have beaten the market twice in a row. After twenty-five coin tosses, there are still fifteen investors who have beaten the market 25 years in a row – and by pure luck. Our problem is that we think of twenty-five years as a long time. And it is when we consider our life spans. The important issue is whether this is a long time relative to the number of investors in the market. And unfortunately, the answer there is no.

But fifty years? Even with ½ billion investors, no one can beat the market fifty years in a row, right? Actually, no one has. Most of Warren Buffett's extraordinary record came in the first few years of his career. The last few years have been pretty mediocre – you might as well have invested in a passive index fund.

Early success matters. Suppose two players, Warren and Ellen, flip a quarter once every day and bet on heads and tails respectively. Warren is ahead at any point in time if there have been more heads up until that time while Ellen is ahead if there have been more tails up till that time. Although each player is equally likely to be in the lead at any given time, it can be shown statistically that one of them will be ahead almost *all* the time. If there have been 1,000 flips, the chances of Warren (or Ellen) being ahead more than 90% of the time is much higher than that she has been ahead between 45% to 55% of the time.

The overall conclusion from the academic research was that markets were pretty efficient in the semi-strong-form as well. Most event studies found that the market reacts correctly to news. There were no systematic over- or under-reaction patterns, and therefore no easy trading rules. Even highly skilled investors using public information (mutual fund managers) did not appear to make abnormal profits.

Finally, a strong efficient market incorporates all information, public or private, about a company into its prices. This seems implausible. How can the market incorporate private information, which by definition, no one else knows, into prices? Moreover, if this is true, it would mean that insider trading legislation (which is essentially meant to prevent traders from taking advantage of private information) is completely unnecessary.

To understand how this is possible, let us assume that insider trading is perfectly legal and that the market is strong-form efficient. Suppose you are the CEO of a firm and you are on a boating trip down the river Cam with your chief of information technology.

The CIT, who appears to have a lot on his mind, suddenly blurts out, "You know, you and I have been friends for a long time. I need to tell you that the firm is having huge problems. Our servers have just been hacked, and the hackers have transferred out nearly all the firm's money. I managed to save the last $10 million, and by sheer coincidence I have that money in bearer bonds below my seat on this boat. There is no hope of the company surviving beyond the end of this month. And when we get to the end of this boat ride, I have a cab waiting for me at the docks. The cab will drive me to the airport where I have a private jet waiting to take me to South America. You will never see me again. At the moment, no one knows this but me, and now you." The CIT is a big burly guy, so there is little hope of you tackling him and holding him down.[7] Your cell phone battery is dead. How does this information get into the price?

The answer lies in your actions. Since insider trading is legal, what is the logical thing to do? Since the company is essentially valueless when the news comes out, your best hope is to sell all your shares before the news emerges. The problem is that the moment you call your broker with instructions to sell all your shares immediately at any price, the broker instantly starts thinking, "This is the CEO of a firm who wants to sell all her shares. I don't need to really know what her information is. All I need to know is that this is bad news. And judging by how frantic she is, this is more likely terrible news." So any rational broker will instantly start selling his own holdings in the firm and call all his clients to sell all their shares as well. Even before your shares have sold, all this front-running has effectively dropped the value of the shares to zero. In other words, the information on the actions of the CEO acts as a signal (as in Chapter 6) in inferring the true value of the company.

As you can see, the crucial part of this example lies in identifying the seller as an insider. Unfortunately, this is not always possible. Insiders hide trades, break up trades into smaller amounts, and sell through friends and intermediaries. Hence, research has shown that markets are not strong-form efficient – insiders do make money.

Evidence Inconsistent with Market Efficiency

In the last few years, an increasing amount of research has shown that apparently persistent patterns appear to exist in all sorts of markets – stock markets, futures markets, foreign exchange, bonds, options, real estate markets, and even in sports betting markets. These patterns appear to violate both weak and semi-strong-form market efficiency. Many of these patterns are extremely simple and easy to take advantage of.

For example, calendar effects appear to be prevalent in returns. Average returns differ within the calendar, appearing to be unusually high/low in certain months, on certain days of the month, or even on certain days in the week. The discovery of these calendar effects gave an early impetus to the field of behavioral finance, because they are hard to reconcile with weak-form EMH. Examples of these calendar effects include the January effect (small firms exhibit high returns in January); the Other January effect (as January goes, so goes the rest of the year); the holiday effect (stock returns are high pre-holidays); the Monday effect (stock returns are low on Mondays); the turn-of-the-month effect (stock returns are high around the turn of the month), and the Presidential Cycle effect (U.S. stock returns are higher in periods when Democratic Presidents hold power than when Republican presidents do so). Explanations (tax-loss selling, institutional window dressing, and others) have been proffered for several of these effects, but it is still difficult to explain why these effects persist. In some cases, it has proven difficult to come up with any explanation at all (the Other January effect or the Presidential Cycle effect).

Other examples of violations of weak-form EMH are momentum and reversal patterns. When testing weak-form EMH as in the previous section, if we extend the period of analysis from days and weeks to months, patterns do show up. For example, abnormal returns on individual stocks are positively autocorrelated at a three-to-twelve-month horizon. What this means is that prior winners (measured over a three-to-twelve-month horizon) appear to stay winners over the next three-to-twelve months. Similarly, prior losers (measured over the same horizon) appear to stay losers. This momentum effect is also large – researchers have documented a 15% average annual return difference between high- and low-momentum portfolios. Not much evidence has been found that these are driven by differences in risk.

Interestingly, when we go from months to years, the momentum pattern reverses. At horizons between three and eight years, the autocorrelation in abnormal returns turns negative. In other words, over these longer time frames, prior winners become losers. Similarly, prior losers now become winners.

As a final example, inconsistent with weak-form EMH, researchers have also documented a lead-lag effect in stock returns. In particular, large stocks appear to "lead" small stocks over a horizon of a few weeks. Formally, there is a positive cross-autocorrelation between abnormal returns on large stocks this week and small stocks next week.

Turning now to evidence against semi-strong EMH, researchers have shown that publicly known firm characteristics can be used to predict abnormal returns in the cross-section. For example, size and book-to-market ratio appear to predict returns better than the CAPM beta. Researchers have mixed beliefs on why this difference in predictability exists. For example, Fama attributes it to a bad model problem in that we really don't know how to measure risk. In other words, the CAPM is not the appropriate measure of risk.[8] Other researchers have argued that sorting on these characteristics gives us implementable and profitable trading strategies. This is the basic idea behind contrarian or value-investing strategies. Fund managers look for stocks with market price that is low relative to some measure of fundamental value (such as book value). They form, for example, portfolios based on past book/market ratios, cash-flow/price, earnings/price, and growth in sales ratios. The idea is that firms with high ratios are value firms, undervalued by the market. Hence, buying these firms will earn investors high risk-adjusted abnormal returns.

Other examples of violations of market efficiency have also been shown in other markets. For example, Robert Shiller, who shared the Nobel Prize with Eugene Fama, showed the existence of predictable patterns in housing markets. Many of these anomalies are being used as the basis for trading strategies in these markets. For example, the carry trade is an example of a strategy that takes advantage of an apparent anomaly in foreign exchange markets.

Systematic Investor Biases

Over the last couple of decades, two schools of thought have arisen in finance. The first group, which includes Fama, argues that markets are in fact efficient across all horizons. The predictability of returns we see are driven by inadequate models for risk. The second group, which includes Shiller, argues that markets are not efficient and irrational investors do have an effect on prices.[9]

So which is correct? Recall that there are three scenarios under which markets will be efficient (prices will not be predictable). In the first, all investors are rational and use, for example, a net present value (NPV) analysis to derive the value of securities. In the second, investor biases are not correlated. The same piece of news causes some investors to become optimistic and some to become pessimistic. Finally, in the third, even if investor biases are systematically correlated, there exist some large arbitrageurs who essentially have unlimited funds and horizons. By taking the opposite positions to individual investors, they drive prices back to fundamental values. Therefore, if we can show that any of the three conditions is fulfilled, we should be more likely to conclude that the markets are in fact efficient and these apparent anomalies are just results of bad model problems.

Just from personal reflection, we can probably rule out the first scenario. How about the second? Daniel Kahneman, a cognitive psychologist, won the Nobel Prize in 2002 because he[10] documented the existence of systematic behavioral biases in human beings that caused them to react similarly to information. Examples of these biases included biases on beliefs such as overconfidence, optimism and wishful thinking, representativeness, conservatism, confirmation bias, anchoring, and memory biases. There were also biases on preferences such as ambiguity aversion. Based on these and other biases, Kahneman and Tversky came up with the concept of prospect theory. Prospect theory describes the way people choose between alternatives that involve risk, when they know the probabilities of potential outcomes. Kahneman and Tversky argued that people make decisions based on the potential value of losses and gains relative to a reference point, rather than the final outcome, and that people evaluate these losses and gains using shortcuts or heuristics. Unlike the CAPM, the model is descriptive. It tries to model how people actually make choices, rather than model optimal decisions for investors.

While prospect theory is attractive, practically it suffers from many of the same implementation issues as the CAPM. It is easy to say that investors evaluate choices according to a reference point, but how is that point determined? Recent research has pointed to salient anchors such as the fifty-two-week high stock price, but absent actual trading data, it is difficult to predict anything outside the laboratory. Overall, though it is probably reasonable to say that the second scenario is also rejected.

Limits to Arbitrage

What about the third scenario? Do arbitrageurs have unlimited funds and horizons that allow them to take the opposite side of the trade to individuals and drive prices to fundamental values? Sadly, the answer is no. The problem goes back to the idea of asymmetric information that we examined in Chapter 6.

Most arbitrageurs are not investing their own money. They are managing the money of others. In other words, there is a separation of expertise and capital in a classic principal-agent problem. The principals are the investors, and the arbitrageurs are the agents. The principals face exactly the two problems we highlighted in the Chapter 6: adverse selection and moral hazard. There are hundreds of fund managers all competing for their money. The investors know that some of these will be good and some will be bad.

Suppose now that the arbitrageur has identified a great trading strategy that takes advantage of mispricing. She shorts the expensive security and buys the cheap substitute in a classic long-short strategy. However, though she knows prices will converge in the long run, earning her massive profits eventually, she runs the risk that prices will diverge further in the intermediate term. The cheap substitute might drop in price, earning her a potential margin call. Similarly, the overpriced security might increase further in price, earning her a second margin call. If the manager does not have the funds to meet these potential calls, the position will have to be liquidated, exposing the manager to massive losses precisely when the mispricing is the largest.

Can the manager approach the investors and ask for more funds? The problem is that whatever the manager says will be exactly what the bad managers will also say. For example, if the good manager tells her investors that she has this amazing opportunity that will earn huge payoffs if they just give her more time, the bad manager will also tell his investors exactly the same thing. Faced with no way to distinguish one type of manager from the other, the investor rationally imposes a short horizon on the manager. Both these reasons mean that managers are unwilling to invest too much in correcting mispricing. Hence, potential arbitrage opportunities may go untapped.

Overall, the takeaway from this chapter is sobering. Are markets efficient, or are they not? Recall that market efficiency consists of two parts: for the rest of the finance concepts to be true, prices have to equal fundamental values. For there to be no free lunch, there should be no way to consistently earn excess returns. My personal sense is that the first is incorrect. There are too many examples of situations when prices do not appear to equal fundamental values. However, my sense is also that the second is correct. Given the existence of systematic biases and limits to arbitrage, there is still no free lunch.

So if prices do not equal fundamental values, are we saying that the rest of corporate finance is useless? I would probably say not.[11] There are potentially two ways in which the ideas we have discussed so far still work.

First, most of these anomalies show up in illiquid situations with little trading volume. In other words, when there are lots of investors involved in pricing securities, the market is pretty efficient. This has implications for corporate strategy. For example, attention is important. Keeping your firm in public view helps in efficiently pricing your shares. That is one reason why firms seek analyst attention and are even willing to buy research from research houses to get that attention. In addition, once anomalies are documented, research shows that they diminish rapidly in magnitude as investors take advantage of them.

Second, horizon matters. In the short term, prices may not equal fundamental values. However, most corporate decisions are not made in the short term. A decision to invest in a billion pound factory is a decision that may require horizons of twenty to thirty years. It is difficult to imagine that firms will stay mispriced over these lengths of time. Over the time frame required for most corporate finance decisions, we can probably safely assume that markets are efficient.

Notes

1. Arbitrage has a very precise meaning in finance. An arbitrage is a business transaction that offers positive net cash inflows in some states of the world, and under no circumstance – today or in the future – a negative net cash outflow. Therefore, it is risk-free and effectively a free lunch. Arbitrage is not the same as earning a risk-free return. After all, government bonds do just that, and they are not arbitrage. The reason is that buying safe government bonds requires you to lay out cash today. This is a negative cash flow. Similarly, arbitrage is not the same as receiving money today without a clear obligation to repay. If you are willing to accept risk, you can often receive cash today. For example, insurance companies take money in exchange for the possibility that they may have to pay up in the future. They hope

    that they will not have to pay off the insurance risk, but they accept the possibility that they might have to pay.

2. Unless your day job does, in fact, consist of trying to earn abnormal returns.
3. Abnormal returns are sometimes called excess returns, because they are returns in excess of a benchmark.
4. To economists.
5. See Jeff Somer, "Buffett's Awesome Feat, Revisited," *New York Times*, March 8, 2015, p. BU3.
6. Economists would call this an educated guess, a term we use when we want to say that we're pulling this number out of our hats.
7. Besides, you can't swim.
8. We can keep it consistent with portfolio theory by arguing that if we could measure the market portfolio for example, or measure the risk premium properly, the CAPM would, in fact, be a precise measure of risk. But we can't implement the CAPM properly. So the reason the CAPM beta does not do a good job predicting returns is because we don't know how to compute the inputs to the model properly. Garbage in, garbage out.
9. The Nobel committee solved this conundrum by giving both researchers a Nobel Prize in the same year.
10. Many of his papers were written in collaboration with Amos Tversky who died in 1996. As we noted previously, the Nobel is not awarded posthumously.
11. But then I would, wouldn't I?

8 Wrapping It Up

Learning Points

- The big picture
- What we know and do not know about corporate finance

The Big Picture

We started the book by discussing four perspectives – firms, individuals, financial intermediaries, and governments. Firms need to raise money (the financing decision) and need to spend this money (the investment decision). Individuals need to find investments to give them the highest possible return for the minimum amount of risk. They also need to be sure that managers will not simply steal the capital that they receive as stewards of the firm. Intermediaries need to match borrowers (the firms) with the lenders (the investors). Finally, governments need to make sure that the process is fair. They also need to make sure that there are no damaging externalities – for instance, that actions taken by one group of people do not cause the whole system to blow up.

To address these four perspectives, we have a total of six major ideas. The first idea, that of net present value (NPV), runs throughout the book. The NPV decision rule is used to determine the best investment decision the firm should take. To compute NPV, we need three inputs. The first is the cash flows to the assets. There are four major types of cash flows: single lump sums, annuities, perpetuities, and continuously compounded flows. Every cash flow in finance can be valued using these four formulae. The second (explicit) input is the discount rate. Finally, the third (implicit) input is the level of leverage of the firm.

The discount rate is determined by investors, not the firm. Investors use the second idea, portfolio theory and the capital asset pricing model (CAPM), to determine the discount rate. The idea behind portfolio theory is simply that when we combine securities into portfolios, some risk disappears because of diversification. The only risk that does not disappear is system-wide risk. The CAPM tells us the price of that risk.

The optimal level of leverage within the firm is given by capital structure theory, which is our third major idea. In a perfect world, without taxes, lawyers, or bankruptcy costs, capital structure theory tells us that the financing structure of the firm does not matter. Once we introduce taxes, lawyers, and bankruptcy costs, one capital structure story tells us that firms trade off the tax benefits of debt against potential bankruptcy costs. This is called trade-off theory. An alternative capital structure story focuses on asymmetric information. It tells us that since cash within the firm has the least amount of asymmetric information associated with it, firms will rely on internal cash before going outside for additional capital. Since debt has the next least amount of asymmetric information associated with it, firms will then choose to rely on debt. Firms will only issue equity as a last resort. This is called the pecking order story. Both stories explain some parts of capital structure but do not explain them completely.

However, firms are not required to make every investment that comes along. In many cases, they have options. These options might be options to expand or options to abandon. We cannot value options using the NPV formula, and our fourth major idea that of option pricing theory, addresses precisely this issue. Option pricing relies on the no-arbitrage principle to a great degree. Pricing any kind of option requires constructing an equivalent portfolio that pays off exactly the same way as the option does. If you know the price of the equivalent portfolio today, we know the price of the option.

All the above four ideas assumed the presence of symmetric information. What that meant was that every party to every transaction had the same level of information. However, that is not a realistic assumption. The last two ideas – asymmetric information and market efficiency – focused on the role that information plays in prices. Asymmetric information analyzes situations in which the parties do not have the same level of information. In this type of situation, the party that is worse off is the party with superior information *and* a superior product. The party with less information knows that he or she has less information and therefore offers the average price. The party that is better off is the party with superior information and an *inferior* product. So asymmetric information situations typically involve a party that is trying to prove to the other side that it is in fact supplying a superior product. The tools it uses to prove its commitment involve signals and screens.

Finally, our last idea, market efficiency, underpins everything else in finance. Market efficiency implies that prices equal the fundamental values that are derived from the NPV formula. It assumes that investors take all possible pieces of information and incorporate them instantaneously into prices. If the market is not efficient, then none of the other six ideas matter. At the moment, there is still some controversy about this last idea. Some researchers believe that markets are perfectly efficient and irrational investors will get driven out of the market. Other researchers believe that irrational investors also help set prices. More research is necessary to resolve this issue.

What We Know and What We Do Not Know about Corporate Finance

There are still huge gaps in our knowledge. For example, we still do not know what risk is. The capital asset pricing model gives us a theoretically elegant way of discussing risk. However, empirically it is impossible to prove the CAPM. Researchers have proposed several alternative asset pricing models to take the place of the CAPM. These are empirically more accurate, but there is no theoretical justification for them. We do not know how firms set capital structure. We do not know whether the markets are really efficient. We do not know to what extent behavioral biases play a role in setting prices.

Even if we did fill in all these gaps, however, it is important to note that most of finance theory discusses individuals and firms in isolation. We do not spend much time discussing how individuals function in society. But individuals and firms do not spend their lives in isolation. We influence and are influenced by other people all the time. How do these links between individuals affect their financial decisions? This area is so new that we do not even know what questions we need to ask, let alone what the answers should be. There are several researchers working with topics like these, but the data are difficult to get, and as yet the results are sketchy, to say the least. Hopefully, time and further research efforts will also help fill in the gaps in both the questions and answers.

Index

Printed in the United States
By Bookmasters